SOCIETIES AND SOCIAL INTELLIGENCE

C. MARGARET HALL

Societies and Social Intelligence *is a guide to discovering the power and complexities of societies and social influences, as well as the impacts they have on our freedom and opportunities. This book is dedicated to readers who want to better themselves, their accomplishments, and the world we live in.*

Table of Contents

The Power and Complexities of Societies

Social Intelligence and Societies

The Power
and
Complexities of Societies

I. Societies and Evolution

One of the broadest views of societies is that they participate in evolution. Because many evolutionary aspects of societies—such as the survival of populations—result from far-reaching forces that are not fully understood, we usually acknowledge that we share our evolutionary heritages with other societies, without knowing much about how our societies changed in the most distant past. It is only in relatively recent historic times that social facts about societies were recorded, together with sporadic commentaries that suggest how societies changed due to natural catastrophes or political reorganizations.

From an evolutionary perspective, history is a fairly modern enterprise which traditionally notes major social events such as wars or leaders' accomplishments. At the same time, modern histories and contemporary analyses frequently underestimate the importance of evolution for societies, with the result that geological and geographical conditions of our original families, kin groups, communities, and societies are not considered as seriously as more recent circumstances.

Mass education has allowed more people to understand that millions of years of evolution impacted early societies and social changes. However, we continue to have scant knowledge about how evolutionary conditions changed the earliest stages of development of communities and societies. Consequently, we must persist in putting pieces of this puzzle together, so that we progress in understanding our pasts, present, and future, even though we are not yet able to delve sufficiently deeply into our evolutionary beginnings.

Given these limitations, we must largely imagine what our earliest societies were like through referring to selected facts that document evolution. Because of the many lacunae in our knowledge of evolution, social intelligence helps us to understand what some of the most significant patterns in evolution appear to be. For example, social intelligence heightens our awareness of the changing power and complexities of societies through time, particularly with regard to individuals, families, communities, cultures, historic social changes, and social justice.

Social intelligence shows us that when we focus on these social perspectives, we can identify varied trends in evolution, history, and globalization, as well as in past, present, and future societies. In this respect, social intelligence guides us in facing and dealing with existential challenges like articulating more clearly how even a limited knowledge of evolution can enlighten us about choosing effective social means to create improved societies.

Because human brains evolved at the same time that societies evolved, we can at least consider that human and social capacities to think effectively are critical for determining the survival of specific groups and societies, as well as individuals. For example, our shared lack of physical strength often requires us to survive through thinking, by assessing the limits we face, and by articulating our preferred goals and ideals. Thus, social intelligence requires us to be more critically selective in choosing how we deal with complex social situations and the everyday social contexts of our lives.

Focusing on evolution necessarily calls into question our beliefs about the nature of human nature and the nature of the universe. Social intelligence shows us that we make choices in adapting to our environmental circumstances, and that we must deliberately choose to survive and be fulfilled if we are to withstand and deal with evolutionary hazards or dilemmas. In these respects, social intelligence enables us to recognize the importance of evolution in our lives, as well as the particular circumstances of our own evolutionary situations.

Given these evolutionary realities, social intelligence suggests that we must choose to be either relatively active or passive, such as by speaking our minds or holding our peace in particular social situations. For example, we choose to be leaders or followers, as well as choose particular goals. We may decide to be engaged individuals, who welcome the next stages of evolution, or isolated beings who retreat from recurring challenges to create social conditions that lead to peaceful co-existence in our complex modern societies. Furthermore, we can opt to be more fulfilled by making socially intelligent contributions to others which create better societies.

Social intelligence requires us to understand ourselves more deeply by looking at the broadest evolutionary dimensions of our being. What is the nature of human nature? What existential demands result from being creatures of evolution? To what extent do relentless evolutionary forces move us along in ways we do not choose? Is it possible to have some degree of control over our societies, or are we so determined by impersonal evolutionary influences that our choices cannot be meaningful?

Societies and Social Intelligence helps us to put these important issues in perspective, so that we let go of evolutionary forces that we cannot control, at the same time that we seize opportunities to go with or against some of the evolutionary aspects of current social changes that engulf our societies. We also assess social facts that suggest that our emotions express significant aspects of our evolutionary development, in order to gain more control over our life chances and social outcomes.

Social intelligence helps us to live productively with many aspects of evolution, history, and globalization that we do not currently understand, and helps us to make as much sense as possible out of these influences at least some of the time. We cultivate a stronger general sense of what evolution means with regard to the qualities of our human and social experiences, for example, knowing that we will not fully understand the power and complexities of the infinite aspects of evolution. In light of these limitations, social intelligence shows us how to choose to be awake and alert to evolutionary choices and possibilities, rather than retreat from these challenges, with the result that we stay ignorant or unfulfilled.

Individuals

As individuals it is all too easy to conclude that we are not affected by societies or evolution, and that whatever we think or do will not influence societies or evolution directly. For example, we are so much in awe of the power of our societies and evolution—which usually magnifies our senses of powerlessness—that we withdraw from societies and evolution rather than respond to them thoughtfully. It is easer to go with the flow of our daily lives than to consider weighty matters such as societies and evolution.

Social intelligence helps us to overcome this powerlessness and ineffectiveness by making us more aware that we inevitably participate in both our societies and evolution. Our interactions with our societies and evolution define who we are and what we accomplish, in that we must adapt to our broadest social environments and social contexts if we are to survive.

Social intelligence requires us to consider how individuals express their uniqueness in modern societies as well as evolution, which define self differently through time. Even though our lived experiences suggest that it is primarily through our societies that we express our individuality, rather than through evolution, it is important to see our human uniqueness in relation to evolutionary origins and development if we are to strengthen our contributions to the common good and social justice.

When we decide to be more socially intelligent, we enhance our effectiveness in both societies and evolution. We increase our understanding of the power and complexities of societies, for example, and become more skilled in adapting actively rather than passively to whatever social circumstances occur. Our social intelligence is expressed through our more enlightened actions, which enhance our achievements as individuals and members of societies. Furthermore, as we deepen our understanding of ourselves in these ways, we understand others more fully.

Social intelligence does not allow us to ignore the importance of understanding ourselves as individuals. For example, we need social intelligence to heighten our awareness of being individuals before we can make truly satisfactory contributions to the common good. Furthermore, we know ourselves more adequately as individuals when we see the power and complexities of our lived connections to evolution, especially through our families, communities, cultures, and social changes.

Even though we cannot be sure that we understand what the nature of human nature is, considering ourselves as individuals who are influenced by evolution allows us to appreciate basic human and social characteristics such as our brains or our emotions. For example, our brains have evolved more rapidly than any other aspects of our bodies. Our brains have also become disproportionately large in relation to our body size, and in relation to the individual and social characteristics of other mammals. These physiological dimensions of our lives suggest that our brains are needed to adapt effectively to our increasingly complex social worlds.

One response to this over-simplified view of evolutionary influences in our everyday lives as individuals is that we benefit from examining how we use our brains, and how we depend on our brains and thinking for our survival and fulfillment. For example, are there constructive and destructive ways of using our brains? Also, how do we make the wisest choices and decisions about using our brains? Can we learn to clarify our thinking, so that we benefit ourselves and others by considering the consequences of achieving our goals?

When we use social intelligence principles to guide our thoughts, our actions move us more easily in constructive directions. Although it is possible to use social intelligence for evil or destructive purposes, negative goals are not considered in *Societies and Social Intelligence*. The assumption here is that it is ultimately in individuals' and societies' interests to use social intelligence for constructive social changes whenever possible.

Making the most of our brains through developing social intelligence helps us to make effective evolutionary adaptations, as well as contribute to societies. Social intelligence shows us how not to be overwhelmed by evolutionary and societal processes, by empowering our individual and collective thoughts, goals, and actions. For example, we matter as individual members of societies, and we play significant parts in evolutionary processes as individuals. Thus, social intelligence shows us how to express our good intentions as individuals, so that we fortify both better societies and evolution through our everyday actions.

Families

Before we can more fully understand what it means to be individuals in evolution or societies in evolution, we must consider how families, communities, and cultures contribute to the power and complexities of societies through time. Participating in our own families, as well as observing different aspects of family dynamics among several generations, helps us to appreciate our human and social interdependence in evolution.

Families are our original societies. In their earliest forms our families are tribes, clans, or kin groups, rather than the modern fragmented nuclear families of parents and children. In these original families each individual child born into a tribe, clan, or kin group is to some extent supported and shielded from harsh environmental conditions by members of older generations. This made survival possible for some of the children who live through the hazards and stresses of their births and early childhood.

It can be surmised that the necessities of family adaptations to harsh environmental circumstances preoccupy most family members, because families' security and resources have to be negotiated each day. These urgencies reinforce the intensity of emotional dependence among kin members, which still exists in hostile environments in modern societies. In fact, we have by no means evolved out of this family emotional dependence in modern societies, even though immediate goals of survival may not be as pressing as in earlier stages of human and social evolution.

Social intelligence is built on the foundation of our working knowledge of families, and social intelligence views family interactions as foundations of our social institutions and cultures. For example, our understanding of both evolution and societies depends on our own experiences of family interdependence, because family interdependence is at the core of our individualities, identities, and social connections with others. Social intelligence helps us understand these powerful emotional processes more fully, so that we gain some control over our interdependent, collective destinies.

Families are long-lasting as small groups in societies, and they are the only small groups which are characterized primarily by their lifetime memberships. Families are based on deep allegiances because they meet our most basic human needs for survival from birth to death, which makes them distinctive and qualitatively different from other groups and social institutions.

The power and complexities of families underlie the power and complexities of societies. For example, when we understand our families more fully, we are better able to decipher widespread patterns of behavior and institutional arrangements in societies. Furthermore, social intelligence helps us to appreciate the evolutionary fact that societies need families in order to survive. We see that social dependencies persist throughout evolution to the present, regardless of the social fact that our primal individual and social needs have been reinterpreted by religions, political rhetoric, and ideologies throughout history.

In spite of shifts in gendered responsibilities in contemporary societies, which have increased balance and cooperation in parental obligations for child care, we continue to invest both realistic and unrealistic emotions in our families and societies. However, social intelligence shows us that we can carve out more emotional freedom in relation to our families' basic emotional imperatives, such as child care, when we are selective in how we cooperate with social influences in our families, societies, and evolution.

It is only with some degree of objectivity or detachment from our evolutionary and emotional states of being that we can think sufficiently clearly about our present social situations and responsibilities. For example, we use our social intelligence more effectively for making constructive social changes and increasing social justice, after we use emotional forces in evolution to achieve more meaningful interdependence in our families.

Our families connect us to our earliest stages of evolution, as well as to refined ways of being in our personal and intimate relationships. We pass on to members of our youngest generations what we learned best in our families, with strong hopes that these youngsters will become fully contributing members of their communities and societies. When we use social intelligence to assess the webs of interdependence and connections in which we are all enmeshed, we clarify our visions of what is possible for our societies' futures within evolution. For example, becoming historical actors by increasing our social intelligence means that our basic knowledge of human and social interdependence launches us into societies, rather than traps us in our families' emotional dependencies.

Communities

Social intelligence shows us that it is useful—even critical—to consider different stages of societies' development in human and social evolution. These reflections on evolution suggest that after family, tribal, and kinship groups survived as small groups of hunting and gathering societies, pastoral economies and horticultural or agricultural practices became foundations for small communities.

Insofar as family, tribal and kinship groups did not disappear from our earliest societies—often becoming more distinctive or more easily recognizable small groups—communities developed from the increasingly settled and stable food-producing patterns of social organization. Gradually, whole societies encompassed many different communities, which had increasingly complex connections among each other, as well as different levels of awareness of themselves as integral parts of societies.

In these respects, communities can be thought of as significant components of our complex societies—including modern industrial societies—in human and social evolution. However, although communities continue to be powerful local groups in our earliest traditional societies, as well as in our earliest historical societies, they are often not as visible in contemporary modern societies. The relatively recent dominance of economic and political forces in industrially advanced mass societies, as well as in globalization, has weakened the local and social conditions necessary for sustaining communities.

Social intelligence suggests, especially in relation to social justice, that optimal conditions for successful adaptations in human and social evolution include preserving or restoring communities as important influences in our complex modern societies. Some aspects of the basic social organization of early societies show us how communities support families and individuals, so that the roots of broader societies are more secure in achieving life satisfaction—as well as survival—for their members. For example, the most effective achievements of communities in historical societies, as well as in complex and powerful modern societies, include more balanced work and family relations, or increased sustenance during crises in individual and family life cycles.

Although historical facts about communities reveal significant abuses of social class privileges, extreme poverty, and sexual exploitation which must not be ignored, it is practical to remain somewhat idealistic in our understanding of social evolution. For example, it is humanly possible for communities to be significant sources of equality, inclusiveness, diversity, cooperation, and openness. Furthermore, we see that strengthening our communities reduces widespread destructive social conditions—such as poverty—that increase alienation.

Communities are also significant because they help us to assess qualities of life in societies. When we formulate goals to improve our communities, for example, we see that our communities necessarily influence our societies and social evolution. To the extent that our communities are humane and meet basic human needs, our societies assume similar ways for people to relate to each other. Even though social policies are indispensable for accomplishing the well-being of all members of societies, when communities provide strong supports, the common good of societies serves more human needs.

Increasing our understanding of social evolution motivates us to restore the most beneficial purposes of communities in evolution and history. Social intelligence shows us the importance of addressing local grass-roots needs, as well as national political concerns, in our modern complex societies. We restore balance and create more powerful social roots, for example, when we pay attention to the health and well-being of communities as well as individuals and societies.

Social intelligence also shows us that social justice is more likely to be achieved when we increase the well-being of our communities. For example, when we are socially intelligent we have effective starting points to formulate our work as historical actors, especially when we let social intelligence guide our decisions and actions toward achieving our preferred goals to increase the common good.

Communities are often our most viable arenas for applying principles of social intelligence—such as providing high quality education for all—because our societies are too complex, too difficult, or impossible to tackle in the short run. Also, because our families originally provided ways to interact with our communities, we are often familiar with how communities react to what we do. Furthermore, we can use our knowledge of families' emotional systems to predict and deal with community members' interests, when we try to build new communities or meet community needs for social justice.

Cultures

Another way to understand the power and complexities of societies in evolution is through our cultures. Due to the vastness of the time periods considered in geological time, the limited physical evidence of human and social life in the earliest stages of evolution can be used only to infer what we think day-to-day life was like at the dawn of civilization. For example, because written historical records did not exist until relatively recently, we necessarily depend on severely limited knowledge about artifacts in our most ancient burial sites for clues about the cultural values of people who lived in families and communities in our earliest societies.

Human remains in early burial sites, together with cultural objects that suggest individuals' wealth and prosperity, help us to build some knowledge about different social classes, contrasts in resources, and beliefs in an after-life. However, for the purposes of increasing our social intelligence, it is often not as important to examine the physical properties of cultural artifacts found close to former living quarters or in burial sites, as to interpret the cultural uses and meanings of the objects found. For example, we reconstruct what daily life was like from limited cultural evidence, rather than solely compare and contrast the cultural artifacts of individuals, families, and communities.

Artifacts from collective living quarters and burial sites suggest the power and complexities of the social and cultural sources of our earliest societies. Whatever the wealth of individuals, families, and communities, people are often compelled to adapt to harsh living conditions. Cultural evidence also suggests that groups found solace and comfort in shared beliefs about the meaning of life, their social achievements, and their personal relationships. Consequently, social intelligence draws our attention to the social fact that our earliest individuals and groups created beliefs to provide meaning, stability, and hope in their uncertain lives.

Social intelligence deepens our understanding of individuals, families, and communities in evolution and

I. Societies and Evolution

societies by showing us how powerful cultures are in meeting basic human and social needs. However, evolutionary needs do not disappear through time, but rather we discover increasingly innovative ways to meet these needs, so that we continue to adapt successfully to our current evolutionary conditions. Whatever cultures exist in our societies, our most deep-seated concern is to adapt to social circumstances and other people in complex evolutionary processes.

When we examine the earliest social origins of our cultures, we appreciate more fully how cultures have evolved in relation to physical and physiological aspects of human and social evolution. Nevertheless, we are who we are today not solely because of the development of cultural objects and cultural resources, but because of how our thinking responds to continuously shifting evolutionary, social, and cultural processes. For example, our thinking derives from evolution as well as formal and informal education based on social and cultural knowledge.

The most refined aspects of contemporary cultures in our most modern societies—and in global societies—have relatively simple evolutionary beginnings as cultural tools, weapons, artifacts, and beliefs. Because we are human beings in evolution, we are still driven—or inspired—to increase cultural meanings in our lives, so that we can live more fully and provide for others more productively.

Social intelligence helps us to identify and define the evolutionary origins of our complex cultures and complex societies. Denying the importance of evolution limits our appreciation of the nature of human nature, and leaves us with narrow rather than rich understandings of the here and now, as well as the past and future. By contrast, when we commit ourselves to increasing our social intelligence, we ponder the evolutionary sources of our cultures more deeply, and make decisions about our current complex social realities based on this information.

Seeing cultural dimensions of evolution sheds light on what we can envision as constructive social changes in our societies. Better futures become possible because we are willing to stretch our minds to encompass more ways of being and taking action than are readily apparent in today's complex societies. Social intelligence adds depth to our perceptions, so that we can choose to be active participants in evolution today, in order to greet and embrace our evolutionary conditions of the present and future more fully.

Constructive Social Changes

Understanding individuals, families, communities, and cultures in evolution clarifies some of the power and complexities that exist in our societies. Also, when we are socially intelligent, we try to assess critical consequences of the major social influences of families, beliefs, social classes, cultures, and societies in evolution, so that we can trace the impacts of these major social influences on our lives today, as well as in the past. These influences are markers that help us to define our priorities in making constructive social changes for societies.

Evolution has many complex levels of social changes, which take place whether or not human beings deliberately participate in evolutionary processes. Consequently, an important existential issue is the extent to which human beings can make direct contributions to evolutionary changes, given the fact that these changes often seem to occur regardless of the impacts that human beings have on societies and social changes. From our own experiences of history, however, it appears that even in relatively short time-spans such as one or two hundred years, human beings can have significant effects on their societies and how societies evolve.

Social intelligence in *Societies and Social Intelligence* focuses on only the constructive social changes that social intelligence inspires, particularly with regard to increasing social justice. For example, social intelligence makes us more aware of the responsibilities we share in creating constructive social changes, as well as the parts we play in increasing societal possibilities that constructive social changes occur. However, social intelligence also teaches us not to take for granted the idea that evolution creates constructive social changes gradually, or that human beings will necessarily choose to make constructive social changes.

Because social intelligence is based on knowledge about some of the individual and social effects of the five major social influences of families, beliefs, social classes, communities, and societies, scrutinizing these social sources helps us to respond creatively to the social situations and social pressures that we face daily. Consequently, socially intelligent action may be thought of as being largely synonymous with creating constructive social changes, especially because being an historical actor increases the effectiveness of those constructive social changes we want to accomplish the most.

When we aim to be socially intelligent through participating in constructive social changes that make real differences in our societies, we gain control over some aspects of evolution. For example, we are no longer victims of evolutionary processes when we are socially intelligent, in part because we are more selective in our decision-making, as well as in choosing which goals to pursue. Our social intelligence thrives from our well-considered choices, which include cooperating with evolutionary forces we think are constructive and productive for our purposes.

Social changes which result solely from evolutionary influences necessarily include what we consider to be both destructive and constructive social changes. For example, social class interactions may establish destructive social inequalities that persist for many generations, thereby limiting opportunities and possibilities for large numbers of people within and among populations. Given these unfortunate facts of evolution and evolutionary changes, one challenge of social intelligence is to become more aware of how to do whatever we really want to accomplish for others as well as ourselves. For example, social intelligence helps us to resist some automatic evolutionary changes, especially those which harm or limit the freedom of individuals and groups.

Surrendering our individual and collective wills, so that we accept all kinds of social changes, places too much trust in evolutionary forces. We cannot control our futures when we operate with such abandon. As significant and powerful as evolutionary processes are, they are only our starting points for understanding the power and complexities of societies today. Social intelligence makes us more aware, so that we become more deliberate historical actors who apply social intelligence to solving current problems and social issues in our societies.

We cannot afford to be indiscriminating in our everyday choices and decisions, because this ultimately restricts our destinies. By contrast, when we heighten our awareness of our options and the consequences of our actions, we are more effective agents in evolution. We become more adept at selecting constructive goals for the common good, as well as make decisions which increase social justice.

Social Justice

As in the case of constructive social changes and the common good, social justice is not directly connected to evolutionary changes as are individuals, families, communities, cultures, and societies. Like constructive social changes, social justice expresses human value choices. We must also actually decide to create constructive social changes, or decide to increase social justice. However, we cannot accept constructive social changes or social justice in the same way that we are obligated to accept evolutionary changes, often because we believe that we cannot control or influence many aspects of evolutionary changes.

Both constructive social changes and social justice are values or ideals which we may choose to guide how we act. For example, we deliberately choose to make constructive social changes or pursue social justice within the context of the broad impersonal evolutionary changes in our societies. At the same time that we choose to increase social justice, however, we cannot afford to deny the realities of evolutionary changes. Whatever we decide, in relation to constructive social changes and social justice, involuntary evolutionary changes within and among societies persist as powerful and complex social processes in their own right.

Social intelligence shows us that we can make real, meaningful differences in broad patterns of social behavior and trends when we select goals which contribute directly to the common good and social justice. From this perspective social justice is a particular kind of constructive social change, which moves us to address moral and social issues about equality, inclusiveness, diversity, cooperation, and openness. By contrast, the moral tone of constructive social changes is less apparent and often less integrated in long range goals, because constructive social changes focus on solving immediate or tangible social problems and social issues in our complex, powerful societies.

In many respects deciding to expand our social intelligence requires us to examine our evolutionary origins, especially with respect to assessing the assumptions we routinely make in our day-to-day understanding of the nature of human nature. How social are we as human beings? What does interdependence mean within our families, communities, cultures, and societies? How can we come to terms with the five major social influences of families, beliefs, social classes, cultures, and societies in relation to our societies and evolution?

When we try to understand some of the scope and depth of the ways in which evolution has impacted our lives and how we think, we see that our emotional roots are found in patterns of interactions in families, beliefs, social classes, cultures, and societies. For example, without our societies and these five major social influences we would not be who we are. Also, without a viable working knowledge of evolution we may tend to either underestimate or overestimate our capacities to act freely and use wise judgments in pressured social situations.

If our socially intelligent approach to understanding the evolution of our societies leads us to accept humans as intrinsically social creatures, can we then assume that people reflect on their behavior to find meaning and purpose in their lives? Can we escape the moral issues of our day, or are we basically compelled to make moral judgments about the everyday qualities of our lives and the lives of others? Do we contribute more or less to the common good or social justice in spite of ourselves, without realizing that this is so? Is social justice a predictable result of our everyday behavior which we should not ignore?

Social intelligence makes us more aware of these issues and tendencies about human behavior in evolution. Our rapidly evolving brains allow us to reflect and become more aware of our missions as individuals and societies, for example, but at the same time we must deal with our ongoing individual and social needs because we are interdependent human beings. Evolution shows us that we are often at the mercy of strong life and death forces in the universe, however aware we are of social justice issues and goals.

In light of these harsh realities, we can choose to educate ourselves by increasing our social intelligence, even though we remain at the mercy of powers that we usually experience as being beyond our human and social capacities. Sometimes becoming religious, for example, provides us with practical ways to believe and act that overcome our feelings of helplessness or hopelessness. In addition, gaining autonomy through social intelligence increases our choices, and motivates us to move forward with agendas that transcend or respond constructively to our given human and social predicaments in evolution.

II. Societies and History

History is a more manageable social change perspective for understanding societies than evolution. Formal education familiarizes us with historical analyses rather than evolutionary assessments, in part because we experience more dynamics of history than evolution during our lifetimes. However, social intelligence requires that we consider both evolutionary and historical perspectives on societies in order to cultivate broad views of societies. For example, we benefit from seeing evolution and history as juxtaposed, or as series of interrelated social changes. These vistas nurture our social intelligence, so that we use social intelligence principles more effectively to guide our everyday decisions.

Whereas evolution encompasses the broadest universal physical and social influences on societies, history is essentially cumulative human records of individual and social events through time. As evolution proceeds, and as history happens, we see the complexities of our societies as varied social changes and globalization. For example, our societies are less isolated now than in previous eras, so we are forced to come to terms with our complex interdependence on familiar and unfamiliar others, if we are to survive and be fulfilled.

In order to consolidate histories of our societies or communities, we assume the perspectives and world views of insiders to some extent. We understand more nuances in social and political events, if we assess and interpret the historical meaning and significance of these events. Furthermore, our views are more compelling to others when we have experienced some of the social or political tensions that we are assessing, and when we understand broad pictures of current events in both historical and evolutionary perspectives.

Writing or interpreting history increases our social intelligence. If we compare patterns of behavior during long periods of time, for example, we clarify our senses of which social influences are strongest in the major dynamics of social changes within and among our complex societies. Becoming sufficiently objective to record or discuss these views of social change allows us to question how we participate in broad social realities through time.

A practical way to make historical assessments of our societies is to see our life histories as being directly related to our families, communities, cultures, and societies. Historical views of our lives describe and explain many different aspects of our behavior, and we are able to think more historically—as well as make more long range decisions and commitments—when we associate the qualities of our lives with local or national events and trends. Our thinking is strongly influenced by political situations like civil unrest or wars, for example, because we cannot escape the impact of these influences on how we conduct our lives.

One of the endpoints of increasing our social intelligence is to become more aware historical actors. To the extent that we are all exposed to past and present historical influences, each person is an historical actor. When we continue to deliberately increase our social intelligence, we give this social fact a high priority in our thinking, decisions, and actions. Although we do not necessarily become aware historical actors in the early stages of increasing our social intelligence, being an aware historical actor is a predictable consequence of increasing our social intelligence.

History is necessary for understanding the power and complexities of societies because it helps us to coordinate our views of past, present, and future societies. For example, socially intelligent historical actors deliberately coordinate past, present, and future social realities, so that they can use vision, focus, and ideals to guide individual and collective social changes. Moreover, examining the breadth and depth of societies through time sustains our objectivity, and strengthens our capacities to choose constructive social changes for societies.

History is an essential means to increase our social intelligence and to bring about effective social changes in societies. For example, we cannot assess the value of particular social changes without looking at historical developments of societies, groups, or individuals. Social facts emerge when we use historical perspectives, and when our assessments of social realities are grounded in social facts, we take more responsible individual and collective actions.

History measures our lives and opens or closes opportunities in societies. This is largely why we need to pay close attention to our enmeshment in historical influences, especially as individuals, families, and members of communities or cultures. After deepening our understanding of historical social facts, we use social intelligence principles to make enlightened social changes which increase social justice.

Individuals

Because we experience history differently as individuals, it is important to understand our life histories in the contexts of our families, communities, and local and national histories. Variations in individual histories are often strongly influenced by broad trends, for example, and we see only part of the broader picture of our lives if we concentrate solely on our inner responses to our immediate surroundings, rather than pay attention to the broader networks of influences in which we are immersed.

Our life history experiences need to be located as precisely as possible in historical trends, because these connect us to our complex, powerful societies. For example, we benefit from knowing to what extent we act autonomously in relation to our peers, or as integral parts of ongoing trends in those groups with which we identify the most. We also need to consider whether we conduct our lives freely, or are caught up with others' expectations, actions, and preferences.

In the final analysis we are individuals amidst the complex masses of families, beliefs, social classes, cultures, and societies. These major social influences shape our understanding of self and others, as well as our world views and what we think we can accomplish. Seeing how families, beliefs, social classes, cultures, and societies have influenced our individual and societal histories helps us to assess our free or restricted behavior in relating to ourselves, others, and our societies.

We get more in charge of our lives when we ponder our behavior in historical contexts. This helps us to increase our social intelligence, so that we can be more responsible historical actors in dealing with evolutionary forces and the more immediate ongoing pressures of everyday life. When we are connected to histories of our circumstances, we are more objective in how we conduct our lives, and more enlightened in our decisions and commitments to increase the common good and social justice. Thus, being socially intelligent means that we examine histories of our social contexts whenever possible, so that we maintain broad social perspectives in assessing what our most strategic actions are.

In order to come to terms with the strong impacts of families, beliefs, social classes, cultures, and societies on our lives, we use historical approaches to understand the depth and consequences of their influences. For example, we may compile family histories in order to understand our personal and political histories more fully. We also trace the histories of our varied beliefs, so that we can assess how useful our beliefs are, and how to let go of our unproductive or contradictory beliefs. Histories of social classes, juxtaposed with our experiences of race and gender, for example, reveal critical ways in which race and gender have influenced us over time. Similarly, histories of our cultures and societies enliven our understanding of the most powerful broad social influences that affect our lives.

History is a useful way to assess the social characteristics of any given situation. For example, we use history to gather what we consider to be the most significant social facts about our concerns. Furthermore, reviewing social facts over long periods of time gives us clues about how to assess social changes, and how to accomplish social changes. Thus history is a vital stepping stone to getting where we want to go in relation to our most cherished goals.

History puts us in touch with major dynamics of the last century. We are often aware of our individual life courses, as well as our stages of development, at the same time that we move through conventional life cycle expectations in our complex societies. Furthermore, our social positions in societies result from social rankings and particular cultural possibilities linked to our social statuses. For example, our life chances are strongly impacted by our genders and races, as well as social classes. Consequently, social intelligence helps us to neutralize some of our social class limitations through examining personal and societal histories of our genders, races, and social classes.

Our broadest views of history merge into evolutionary perspectives, and help us to see patterns of interactions that characterize our pasts, present, and futures. If we focus on becoming historical actors through increasing our social intelligence, we understand the historical conditions of our pasts, identify the most significant ways to construct history in the present, and envision improved futures more clearly. History is made up of continuously powerful social influences, which open up individuals' possibilities for the present and future.

Families

It is important to consider families as relatively closed small groups, whose life-time members are drawn from several different generations. Social intelligence shows us that we cannot fully understand patterns of family interactions without considering at least three generations of family members. Our interdependent family connections are traced more easily and more accurately, for example, when we see our modern conventional nuclear families as outgrowths of past generations' patterned relationships.

One way to understand how our families are embedded in our complex societies is to write up or map out our family histories. These histories provide us with clear evidence of the extent to which individual life outcomes are products of family dependencies in the contexts of diverse broad social influences. Our individual, family, community, and national histories are entwined in unique ways, which allow us to see how our beliefs, social classes, cultures, and societies are held in place by families' roots.

Social intelligence places a high premium on understanding family sources of our human nature and orientations to social action. Our family dependencies underpin many of our interactions with others, and our social know-how or social intelligence originates in these early and continuing influences on our thinking and behavior. The main purpose of understanding our families, according to social intelligence, is to get more in charge of our own inclinations and aspirations, so that we lead fulfilling and productive lives.

One way history reveals the impacts of our families on who we are and what we do is the clarifications that family histories bring to family interdependencies, especially those which are repeated through different generations. For example, relationships between spouses or between parents and children tend to repeat themselves—sometimes in generations which seem to be removed from the others, rather than in consecutive generations. Similarly boys and girls may experience the same or contrasting parental expectations among different generations of families.

What is particularly significant here, which reinforces the power of our families, is families' lasting impacts on our emotions, emotional well-being, and vested interests. For example, we usually invest our strongest emotions in activities that mean the most to us. We choose friends and partners among those who have similar interests, and we often feel most comfortable with particular religious beliefs due to past family influences, such as when we originally became religious as children.

Social intelligence helps us to understand the depth and power of our family emotional dependencies, in order to come more into our own by breaking away from family patterns that do not serve us well. Social intelligence teaches us to discriminate between constructive and destructive family emotional processes, for example, so that we are more selective in making decisions and choosing goals.

One way to increase our objectivity about families is to collect historical information about who was dominant or dysfunctional in our families' emotional systems. This allows us to detect more easily the many ways in which these critical patterns are repeated through different generations. When we realize that we could be victims of these repetitions, we are more adept at summoning the energy and will necessary to steer more reliable courses in our lives.

History-making, by collecting social facts about our families, is an enlightening exercise. For example, we can share these historical facts with other family members, or circulate our compiled family histories to them. Although there is no guarantee that our relatives will praise our efforts, they often appreciate the time we take to understand our shared past. As a consequence, we may be depended on more in times of family crises, for example, or we may be included in more family gatherings than before we became family historians.

In the final analysis history places our families in meaningful social contexts, which allow us to understand more fully who we are as individuals. Historical dimensions of our families also put us in closer touch with the lived power and complexities of our societies. Although we may be weakened as well as strengthened by the ways in which we are rooted in our families, we can depend on social intelligence as a reliable guide to ensure that we benefit from our family connections in the long run. Furthermore, once we establish mature interdependent relationships in our families, we participate in other social groups and complex societies more productively. Staying meaningfully connected to our families allows us to be responsible historical actors, who choose goals that increase the common good and social justice.

Communities

Ideally our families are still at least potentially attached to their local communities, even though for at least the last hundred years communities in modern industrial societies have been gradually breaking down and leaving voids in meaningful communications between families and villages, towns, or cities. The growth of suburbia and the general spread of urbanization throughout societies have given rise to new connections for families, especially through recent developments in technologies, travel, and communications. However, these alternatives to communities do not yield the same immediate life-enhancing social support and security that many traditional communities provided historically.

II. Societies and History

In this age of international development, where the world seems to be becoming more of a global village, our global cities—the largest cosmopolitan centers in different societies—may contain varied communities. Due to increased pluralism in our complex modern societies, global cities have spawned rich diverse mosaics of co-existing social classes and ethnicities. In some respects, multicultural centers or peripheral areas in cities resemble earlier local communities, especially where global city cultures change dramatically street by street.

Increasing our social intelligence includes understanding some of the most critical dimensions of power and complexities in our modern societies. We start this complex task by examining recent social changes. Later we find, for example, that human beings still need social supports that go beyond the immediate pressing dependency needs that families strive to meet. However, because history shows us that our traditional community supports continue to erode in the twenty-first century, we need to design alternative ways to create communities or broad social networks that orient us satisfactorily for effective constructive participation in our societies.

Historical perspectives on our changing communities strengthen our social intelligence. For example, we gain fuller understanding of the social consequences of gradual breakdowns of traditional communities, when we at the same time examine the major social influences of families, beliefs, social classes, cultures, and societies through time. This scope of concerns helps us to appreciate the complexities of our human and social needs to survive and be fulfilled in our societies. Consequently, we may become more motivated to contribute to the common good and social justice, by creating new social structures and opportunities for communities that meet the real needs of all.

History helps us to understand which social conditions in our communities need to be perpetuated. We also need to acknowledge that traditional hierarchical communities did not meet the needs of all people in the past, and that some idealizing of this past still goes on in much current thinking about communities. For example, social class divisions in villages and towns frequently increased rigidity in the hierarchies of our traditional communities, so that the living conditions of less privileged groups were extremely inadequate.

Social intelligence considers social facts in historical changes in our communities in order to create optimal conditions for designing future communities. However, rather than emphasize the quality of connectedness in traditional communities, social intelligence suggests thoughts and actions to establish communities that are more egalitarian, inclusive, diverse, cooperative, and open than in the past. For example, we must find ways to reduce alienating conditions fostered by our traditional communities, even alongside these communities' members' good intentions to support each other.

Present-day communities also need to facilitate populations' access to government sponsored social services so that individuals, families, and social classes or ethnic groups are not isolated from each other, but rather develop means to support themselves within communities and societies. These innovative patterns in multiculturalism and diversity respond directly and effectively to our shared dependency needs. Furthermore, our new ways of doing things become blueprints for accomplishing goals differently, through building new foundations for our dying communities. Such deliberately planned measures increase meaning and purpose in people's lives, as well as empower democratic decision-making.

Socially intelligent strategies in complex modern societies reflect current ideals, but may seem impossible to achieve given today's economic and political priorities. However, we will not progress as much as we want to if we continue to ignore populations' needs to use community supports in times of rapid social change. Social intelligence grounds us in these social realities, and guides us in making productive, inclusive goals more achievable as we gradually increase the common good and social justice.

Cultures

Cultures give us important historical perspectives in our social intelligence, as well as deepen our understanding of who we are and what we want to accomplish. Even though cultures vary widely, we necessarily find that we feel more at ease in some cultures than others. For example, although cultures are usually broader in scope than communities, cultures underpin and define all our communities. Cultures reflect whole societies and global trends among different societies, and some of the shared characteristics of cultures include values, ideals, ideas, knowledge, religions, laws, lifestyles, expectations, and world views.

It is important to view cultures historically, in order to understand cultural differences, and how cultural or social changes occur. The dominant values of particular historical eras—such as the Renaissance, the Enlightenment, or the Industrial Revolution—dominate whole societies as well as local regions within societies. Particular trend-setting values may create historical shifts in the patterns of behavior or lifestyles that underpin social institutions and historical events. In these respects, our cultures initiate historical changes throughout our societies and among our societies.

History is more complex than the sum total of social changes related to leaders' accomplishments, because new emphases in values or purposes are often needed to change the course of history. Furthermore, in order for societies to move in new directions, our collective historical awareness has to undergo qualitative changes in addition to accepting new emphases in values and purposes that are expressed and lived by political, religious, economic, or educational leaders in our societies. Our cultures are democratic forces in modern history—the masses of societies' populations determine the currents of culture and social changes in contemporary societies.

Social intelligence helps us to see and understand reciprocities between our cultures and broad social changes, as well as cultures' impacts on entertainment and leisure activities. Although current activities in our most prosperous societies display much cultural hedonism, at the same time thinkers or activists try to break through our mundane repetitive banal worlds with different cultural values, in order to take new directions in knowledge, productivity, and fulfillment. When the cultural values that contemporary cultural leaders espouse resonate with sufficient individuals and groups in societies a quantum leap occurs, that transforms cultural standards and daily achievements.

Social intelligence helps us to understand such feats of effective leadership in societies, together with their social consequences for entire populations. At the same time, social intelligence teaches us to appreciate democratic models of cultural change. For example, when we consider what our cultures are from historical perspectives, we find new opportunities for our own leadership through living according to different values and priorities. We maintain and increase our social intelligence, so that we can design richer cultures and improved futures for our complex societies.

When we re-educate ourselves about societies and cultures by applying historical perspectives to our particular social situations, we expand our world views by incorporating broad visions of new possibilities and new opportunities. For example, social intelligence helps us to understand the critical importance of making high quality education available to all throughout our societies, so that we raise cultural standards and enrich cultural expectations within and among societies.

Social intelligence shows us how our cultures enable us to connect directly with our societies, through being agents of meaningful social and cultural change. We nurture our senses of belonging to our societies through our cultures, for example, even in times of intense political hostilities such as wars. Our cultures allow us to focus on patriotism, and to at least temporarily unify our varied beliefs about what our societies stand for. Thus our cultures essentially hold our societies together, as well as create changes which we understand and interpret through history.

Although history has many dimensions in addition to cultures, cultures guide our interpretations and knowledge of what social events mean. In these respects cultures make history come alive with contemporary purposes and creative directions, which guide societies to establish more meaningful priorities for the future. For example, we may make commitments to save our societies because of the deep cultural meanings that our cultures provide. Ultimately it is our collective respect for the cultures of our societies that is lived as loyalties to our societies through history.

Constructive Social Changes

One of the most important contributions of cultures to our powerful and complex societies is that cultures provide us with critical resources for innovating and bringing about social changes. Given this social fact, social intelligence shows us that we can choose to make constructive social changes in the organization and priorities of our societies, and that history provides us with evidence of the successes and failures of some of these endeavors.

When we turn to history for information about how our societies are organized, or about the priorities our societies have, we find patterns in how populations have adapted in many different situations. Although we like to think that we are in charge of our destinies, especially in modern Western societies, we see that many social influences transcend or overwhelm individual decisions, including the decisions of respected policy-makers or leaders of societies. For example, wars, market forces, and climate changes have been extremely difficult to control throughout history to the present day. We need effective collective political wills in societies, in order to accomplish some of the most difficult or most challenging tasks involved in bringing about constructive social changes.

One of the political and cultural strategies used to accomplish constructive changes in societies is to educate the masses, not only so that populations will be prepared to work productively in both national and global economies, but because they will be more enlightened in making political choices, and in establishing priorities for the distribution of societies' resources. Strengthening the moral compasses of societies in these ways helps us to muster the political will necessary to formulate and implement social policies that meet widespread social needs effectively, and increase the common good.

History not only shows us how early democracies occurred, but also how democracies grew and prospered in a wide variety of settings. Social intelligence encourages us to look at history to find out how democracies can be deliberately cultivated, so that populations can resolve some of the difficult social issues that face them in modern times. For example, we must voluntarily and deliberately work together if we are to deal with the most glaring inequities in our everyday circumstances. We also need to combine our intellectual and material resources, in order to take enlightened actions that remedy our most pressing social ills, such as poverty and the widening social class contrasts in modern societies.

II. Societies and History

One of the most significant goals in today's prosperous countries is to increase the constructive social changes already underway to address existing widespread inequities. We need leaders who will deliberately reach out to those with the deepest needs, for example, and leaders who share their responsibilities wisely with others. We must also learn how to mobilize more of our human resources, in order to resolve our most intractable social issues.

Social intelligence shows us how to use history to learn from our mistakes, so that we are more successful in the present for the future. For example, we need to face current social dilemmas squarely, rather than avoid these challenges. Through maintaining our awareness of the power and complexities of our societies—if only by paying more attention to current news releases and serious news reports—we can be more constructive in our responses to social circumstances than before.

Overall, history shows us that although we have made some progress during human evolution, we have not yet been able to control or bring into being what we intend to change. History shows us that our most revered leaders, as well as our most established social procedures, have fallen short of what we want to achieve. This is why history that is focused solely on the past does not often yield sufficient evidence that populations can make productive social changes in the present.

However, when we consider that most children do not have to labor for wages in many modern societies, or that many women have more meaningful legal rights than before the last hundred years, we see that constructive social changes have occurred. Furthermore, even though legislation that ensures these new freedoms could be reversed, at present this possibility seems remote.

Together with historical evidence of limited constructive social changes in our modern complex societies, social intelligence assures us that whatever behavior is learned can be unlearned. Our social class inequalities, for example, result largely from conditioned learning, and because social classes are not innate, they can be unlearned and reversed when a critical mass of people wants these changes to occur. Thus our knowledge of history and social changes encourages us to use our social intelligence to make constructive social changes in our complex and powerful societies in the present for the future.

Social Justice

History reveals how different beliefs or new legislation can make fundamental changes in how all members of populations are treated, as well as in who has opportunities to better themselves during their lifetimes. However, some historical patterns of increased opportunities during a lifetime may not be what are experienced by many members of populations. For example, examining intergenerational family dynamics—through extended family histories and social histories—shows us that it is generally members of younger generations that experience more real changes in their life circumstances than members of older generations. This means that what is relatively new in modern societies is that increased numbers of young people manage to change their circumstances during their own lifetimes than was possible in earlier time periods.

Social justice is a social ideal that prompts us to be aware of people's suffering in societies, and invites us to do what we can to prevent or neutralize this suffering. For example, we need to have empathy for others in order to commit ourselves to social justice goals, and the understanding that social intelligence gives increases the likelihood that we will both develop and use our empathy. Consequently, when we understand the power and complexities of our societies, we are more enlightened in our views, and more competent at realizing our social justice goals.

II. Societies and History

History helps us to see patterns in social justice that trace legislation as a common source of the better quality of life available to many people in modern societies. Laws which narrow extreme differences between the life chances of members of upper and lower classes improve satisfaction throughout societies, because when one part of society is strengthened, the whole society and the world benefit to some extent. This social fact is one reason why each one of us is needed to contribute as much as possible to increasing the common good and social justice in our societies—so that the world will gradually meet widespread social needs more effectively today and in the future.

When we use the past to learn how we should conduct ourselves today for better futures, history becomes a tool for building our practical knowledge or know-how, so that we make real differences in others' lives as well as our own. An historical time-span is considerably shorter than an evolutionary frame of reference, for example, which makes history easier to apply to our everyday situations. Furthermore, thinking historically allows us to note trends in human interventions through time, such as factory laws during the industrial revolution, that have brought about major social changes for different societies. Using historical perspectives confirms that what we decide to do with our resources can be forces for good, and that we are responsible when we undertake tasks that enhance the lives of all rather than privilege a few.

Even though we may not be particularly deliberate in our efforts to increase social justice, as long as we are moving in this general direction, whatever we decide to do will help to reduce others' suffering. Although we could all benefit from increasing our commitments to achieve social justice, thereby increasing social justice through our actions, we risk overemphasizing our social justice intentions, with the result that others predictably criticize or resist our well-intentioned efforts. Rather, being effective means that we should balance our efforts, so that we persuade like-minded others to cooperate with us to achieve our social justice goals.

Suffice it to emphasize here that we need to pay close attention to history and patterns of social change that have occurred throughout history, as well as to how we create history today. Becoming an historical actor—through increasing our social intelligence about the histories of families, beliefs, social classes, cultures, and societies—makes us vigilant about social trends and social consequences. For example, we increase our responsibility for self and others when we act in ways which bring about historical improvements in social trends, because we have achieved meaningful long range changes. Furthermore, we predictably increase our own life-satisfaction when others benefit from our works.

Optimal conditions for increasing social justice are to work cooperatively with others to increase the common good through using historical perspectives. For example, history shows us that effective political and social actions result when individuals work together with those who share similar values and goals. This strategy deliberately expands societies' opportunities by establishing new priorities and new designs to share social resources more widely. Social intelligence shows us that the cost of supporting the status quo is too high, because when we allow history to take its course without enlightened interventions, destructive social consequences follow.

III. Societies and Globalization

Some of the power and complexities of our contemporary societies are more visible today than in the past, partly due to the relatively rapid globalization that has occurred in the last fifty years. At present almost no corner of the world is unexplored, and mass education has enabled many people to be informed about countries and lands throughout the world.

An outgrowth of ongoing trends in globalization is that no country exists in isolation from other societies. Our social interdependence is an increasingly salient fact of our existence and being, and we can no longer deny the importance of our dependence on other societies and others' resources. For example, the division of labor within and among societies is constantly changing, because patterns in material assets and access to substantive means for our survival and fulfillment shift and get more specialized through time. Today some of our most prosperous societies import goods from distant countries, rather than strive to be self-sufficient in their own communities and societies, especially when particular goods and services are scarce or difficult to produce.

Social intelligence helps us to understand the dynamics of our wide-ranging global social needs and patterns of exchanges in international market forces. For example, we understand the local qualities of our social situations more fully when we consider them in broad social contexts, especially with regard to the five major social influences of families, beliefs, social classes, cultures, and societies. The broad perspectives of social intelligence guide us to coordinate our working knowledge of evolutionary and historical changes with ongoing social facts about trends in globalization.

Even though both economies and political forces have been the most dominant moving forces in globalization so far, cultural shifts are also significant, especially with regard to cultural ideals such as social justice. If we are to successfully control some aspects of evolutionary or historical influences in and on our societies through social intelligence, we need to reassess our priorities in light of the ideals and values of social justice, especially if people are to survive and be fulfilled. We cannot continue to support only elitist privileges in the powerful social hierarchies among societies, if all are to benefit from the fruits of education and modern technology.

In order to use social intelligence to examine and intervene in globalization, we first asses how families, beliefs, social classes, cultures, and societies are major social influences in the world at large. Even though we may do little more than scratch the surface of possibilities for understanding the power and complexities of these major social influences, we can see continuities in their patterns of dominance over the qualities of our lives in contemporary times. For example, social classes appear to be less hierarchical in some modern societies, because fewer social classes are now ranked according to economic means or social connections. A relatively new fluidity in contemporary social class identities derives from a wide range of different social classes based on gender, race, ethnicity, education, sexual orientation, and ablebodiedness.

Overall changes in societies created by globalization reflect contrasts in traditional and modern societies, where cultural values either support traditional institutions or motivate us to modify traditional institutions. For example, our shared knowledge about religions has sufficiently multiplied in the last few decades that many people now choose to observe religious practices from several major world denominations, rather continue their commitments to the original religions of their families.

In order to understand the many complex impacts of globalization on societies and vice versa, we examine how individuals are influenced by globalization as well as how families, communities, and cultures are influenced by globalization. We also look at some of the constructive social changes that have occurred in globalization, particularly those which have been constructive rather than destructive in their consequences. This helps us to assess the importance of social justice in shaping globalization, so that we can more seriously consider creating future societies which reflect our most cherished social values.

Social intelligence gives us confidence that the choices that confront us today make interventions in globalization possible. Even though we must think through our decisions as individuals, we need to take globalization influences into account in our day-by-day assessments. Furthermore, we should not shift decision-making responsibilities to governments, in the belief that individuals cannot impact globalization, but rather choose to build on the fact that we are responsible because our decisions and commitments have global consequences.

Individuals

It is largely only within the last hundred years that a critical mass of individuals has pondered and discussed the significance of globalization for the well-being of individuals and whole populations. Until now, issues about globalization were addressed more or less selectively by explorers, politicians, journalists, scholars, and major corporations, who each had contrasting vested interests for understanding how global realities transform our lives.

Today, individuals who are particularly observant or well-educated grasp some significant aspects of the omnipresence of globalization within and among societies, and frequently voice concerns about destructive rather than constructive social consequences of globalization.

In order for complex and powerful societies to be actors in globalization, social intelligence suggests that there must be a widespread heightened awareness of what or who globalization involves, and of how we can be more discriminating in accepting or rejecting globalization in order to protect the well-being of whole populations. Furthermore, it is necessary for us to act collectively if we are to be truly effective in questioning or protesting the powerful impacts of economic, political, and cultural exchanges in globalization.

The breadth and power of globalization easily overwhelms or exploits the uniqueness and vulnerability of particular societies, especially our most traditional societies. Consequently, before we realize it, we may get caught up in global economic, political, or cultural trends which lead to our societies' destruction, rather than meet real social needs through increasing our societies' prosperity and well-being.

Social intelligence counteracts or neutralizes some of the harmful tendencies of dominant global influences to determine important qualities of our lives. For example, social intelligence makes us aware of the powerful impacts of the five major social influences of families, beliefs, social classes, cultures, and societies which underpin economic, political, and cultural forces in globalization.

When we understand how we are subjected to others' goals and intentions through the basic social influences of families, beliefs, social classes, cultures, and societies, we are more able to use the facts of our interdependence to inspire collective actions to increase the common good and social justice. We need not be victims of social circumstances because principles of social intelligence reliably guide us to strengthen our contributions as historical actors, who seek to direct globalization toward meeting real human and social needs more fully.

Even though social intelligence teaches us that we are more effective when we work cooperatively and collectively with others to attain our goals to increase the common good and social justice, we also need to remember that all historical actors are individuals and that all individuals are historical actors. Social intelligence makes us more aware of our potentials as unique historical actors, for example, so that we are not tempted to accept the status quo, or construct world views that are based on passivity rather than enlightened social actions. We understand our own uniqueness as individuals more fully when we are aware of the critical significance of our interdependence, as well as the necessity to formulate a collective will to make the world a better place for coming generations.

Social intelligence teaches us to respect our uniqueness as individuals, because our uniqueness strengthens our capacities to contribute to the common good and social justice. However, at the same time we must acknowledge the many ways in which we depend on others, and others depend on us. We are inextricably interdependent in whatever we want to accomplish, and this makes us more limited in achieving our socially intelligent goals, as well as more prepared to work with like-minded others to increase social justice. Thus, the weakness and vulnerability of our individuality and independence is strengthened rather than destroyed by cooperating with others to achieve shared constructive goals.

We are individuals first, because our lives depend on our personal physiological well-being, but we are also interdependent members of families, communities, cultures, and societies. Moreover, we are individuals within contexts of globalization, rather than individuals defined solely by families, communities, and societies.

Modern times provide us with opportunities to travel and to be educated about wider worlds than our ancestors knew. With these new perspectives and advantages we can now at least aspire to have the best of all worlds as individuals and agents of global change. For example, social intelligence urges us to think through how we want to live in both local and global contexts. Consequently, we do not sacrifice our priorities as individuals to the common good, but rather express our uniqueness more fully through our enlightened participation as both individuals and historical actors in globalization.

Families

In contrast to individuals, families have lives of their own as small groups, which go beyond the particular activities of their individual family members. More than other small groups, and perhaps largely because of families' emotional intensities and their lifetime memberships, families tend to be relatively closed small groups, especially in times of rapid social change and political or personal crisis. For example, family members frequently band together to overcome disruptions caused by rapid social changes or family turmoil.

We can usually see patterns of interdependence in families more clearly than other social groups, and we more easily watch or participate in family adaptations to severe personal crises like the deaths of central players in families' emotional systems. For example, if parents die prematurely in our families, we experience waves of disruption and imbalance for considerable periods of time, until several family members adapt effectively to these severe losses. Social intelligence makes us aware of patterns of interdependence in our families, and families' overall power in influencing our definitions of self and world views.

These characteristics of families make families, as well as individuals, actors in globalization. Our individual well-being is so closely intertwined with our families' well-being that families become crucial decision-makers in globalization. Although families are defined in starkly contrasting ways—including members who are completely unrelated by blood, as well as those who have clear genetic or physiological lineage—families can usefully be thought of as actors who cope more or less successfully with dominant economic, political, and cultural aspects of globalization.

Families who manage to hold their own in the midst of globalization pressures are often families that deal best with the social pressures of their members and their complex, powerful societies. Although it may be difficult to discern the emotional impacts of our own family dependencies, we can see how other families' interactions influence their members' attitudes, priorities, and decisions.

The many complex ways in which our families influence our behavior help us to realize the extent to which families often pressure us to conform to particular attitudes and actions, in order to sustain family memberships. We are who we are in large part due to the ways we interact with our relatives as children and adults. Therefore, it is difficult to escape the depth of the emotional impacts our families have on us, whether we consider our families as key players in globalization or not.

Even though we may acknowledge the power and complexities of our families, and their importance in establishing our basic views of life, we often fall short in recognizing the strength of families' contributions to globalization. Sometimes it takes specific characteristics of families to appreciate that social factors such as travel open up some families, so that they become more active agents in globalization. For example, the widely scattered geographical locations of some family members often increase the flexibility or rigidity of their families' emotional systems, which means that these families are agents of globalization regardless of whatever else they choose to accomplish.

Patterns in scattered family memberships are more clearly seen as aspects of globalization when occasional travel becomes migration, or young adult family members live in foreign countries for long periods of time, sometimes indefinitely. Migrant family members settle into their adopted complex societies, by devoting much of their time and attention to developing different ways to act, as well as new goals to pursue. Thus recent increased trends in the global spread of family members show that individuals and families are participating more in globalization.

In these respects families migrate more easily than communities, which usually have too many local members. Also, because communities do not demand lifetime memberships, they are not as clearly defined agents of globalization as families. However, families continue to have intense emotional impacts on our lives, whether they are geographically scattered in their living and working arrangements or not, and families are also powerful agents of globalization whether or not they realize it.

Diverse family responsibilities suggest other dimensions of globalization in which families participate. For example, many global activities flow from the social fact that some families are more mobile in their outreach to find improved circumstances for raising their children, particularly through striving to be well-educated with rewarding jobs. Moreover, cosmopolitan migrant families also gain social status by showing their achievements in far-off places to other family members.

Although family behaviors often reinforce the power of traditional social class differences, family migrations frequently open up more possibilities for members of younger generations than were realized during the initial migrations. As a result, the social intelligence of families or different family members is increased. Furthermore, members of these families' communities and societies deepen their understanding and respect for social influences, due to relatives' enriched contributions to the common good and social justice.

Communities

Although neither globalization nor communities are identified easily, we can make some worthwhile generalizations about their contemporary social trends and immediate social consequences. For example, recent increases in globalization have made communities more complex, as well as societies. At the same time that urbanization within societies spread, for example, communities with international ties developed in cities, suburbia, and rural settings. Thus, populations in different societies become more diverse as globalization increases, due to frequent international migrations, with the result that considerable enriched diversity in communities and societies is found in cosmopolitan cities.

Because communities grow and develop wherever people live, to the extent that communities can be identified we see that they often become more pluralistic and more inclusive. This shift within communities occurs because the traditional hierarchical structures of established communities cannot withstand either the pressures and needs of particular immigrant groups, or the impacts of rapidly changing populations. In addition, globalization brings its own economic and political influences to bear on communities and populations, so that we develop social conditions that are constantly trying to adapt to the consequences of evolutionary, historical, and global changes.

Given these significant social transitions, and given the everyday needs of individuals and families, a shared hope is that today's communities will be sufficiently flexible to honor pragmatic—but not always popular—values such as equality, inclusiveness, diversity, cooperation, and openness. These values foster social conditions that make more flexible communities possible than the traditional hierarchical structures of historical communities, which are frequently characterized by serious social problems such as prejudice, discrimination, and closure to outsiders.

Social intelligence helps us to understand what these differences in communities mean, as well as helps us to be critical about our communities' strengths and weaknesses in meeting global social needs. Although we may think that the power and complexities of our societies would not necessarily be enhanced by resuscitating traditional communities or by creating new kinds of communities, we must be prepared to deal with many social unknowns when we adapt to changing social realities. Our social intelligence, together with our shared needs to adapt to changing social environments, gradually lead us to design new ways to organize ourselves, so that we add clarity and use broader perspectives in our assessments of how to interact with others each day.

The principles of social intelligence—which underlie our shared hopes for stronger, more adaptive, and more open communities in globalization—derive from the relatively new values or new emphases of equality, inclusiveness, diversity, cooperation, and openness. When we see how these modern, adaptive values make our traditional communities more flexible, for example, we become more motivated to increase the common good by incorporating them into our goals and ways of relating to each other in global contexts. Social intelligence suggests that focusing on making these particular value changes enriches globalization, rather than perpetuates imbalances between hardships and privileges.

Nurturing social intelligence is a reliable way to build flexible communities in globalization. Furthermore, developing social strategies that move us in this direction reduces the likelihood that social conflicts between communities and societies will occur. Ideally, our new communities are sufficiently strong to sustain the complexities of modern societies, so that globalization is more humane. This is due to the social fact that enlightened historical actors work cooperatively to increase the common good and social justice in globalization.

A recurring characteristic of globalization is that global communities develop beyond national boundaries, spreading across different societies as well as within them. These international communities are often built on shared cultures, such as similarities in values related to particular beliefs, social classes, races, ethnic groups, genders, sexual orientations, educational achievements, and ablebodiedness. For example, upsurges in recent Internet exchanges show us that having shared interests is a sufficient basis for global community interactions, even though these exchanges may be virtual international contacts rather than living, ongoing relationships.

Current increases in global travel, sometimes due to widespread low pricing, is another recent aspect of globalization that shows us that international community-building is here to stay, and will continue to enrich our local communities and societies. Social intelligence is a reliable guide for establishing a wide variety of international communities, especially those that aim for constructive social changes and social justice. The principles of social intelligence help us to create a common ethos through our global communities, because values are essential components of all cultures, social classes, and communities. Consequently, when we make commitments to increase our individual and group social intelligence, we necessarily participate in more effective collective efforts to build future societies with improved global social conditions.

Cultures

Cultures pervade globalization and are integral aspects of globalization trends. Cultures are relatively free-floating ideas that are often identified as ideals, values, beliefs, knowledge, laws, religions, meanings, or expectations.

Sometimes—especially in the present—there appears to be little order in our cultures, especially those cultures which result more directly from the reciprocity or give-and-take of globalization.

Even though many people consider cultures to be ways of meeting personal needs to rest, relax, or be entertained in our modern hedonistic societies, mass education has helped us to recognize that cultures are much deeper and more complex than this. For example, it is largely cultures that open doors for value changes, as well as cultures that suggest new ways for societies to organize themselves. Our responses to cultural invitations to change our values express core aspects of our social intelligence. For example, social intelligence orients our thinking and strategic actions toward making value choices to increase the common good and social justice.

We tend to think most clearly when we apply cultural symbols to our understanding of our local and global social situations. Because globalization is international, our world views are more complex to the extent that we learn about societies other than our own. Furthermore, the breadth of globalization—which may overwhelm us—makes us more aware of the power and complexities of all societies.

Social intelligence helps us to be sufficiently objective about globalization that we understand the breadth of complex social influences, and at the same time focus on the five major social influences of families, beliefs, social classes, cultures, and societies. Even though cultures may confuse us, because they are rapidly changing and seem to be disorderly in the many ways they express their complex symbols, they may also clarify cultural diversity by suggesting new patterns and priorities in value choices.

Social intelligence helps us to recognize distinctions among the cultures of individuals, families, communities, and social classes, as well as contrasts in national and international cultures. Our knowledge of what cultures are deepens our understanding of the wide ranges of human nature that are expressed in evolutionary adaptations and historical changes. For example, we are all influenced by the complexities of constantly changing international relations due to economic, political, and cultural pressures in evolution and history.

Our national cultures are particularly important because they give us baselines for comparing cultural well-being among international societies. For example, we assess which cultural values seem to drive most people's goals and ambitions, as well as what we consider to be appropriate resources to provide for the most vulnerable and needy members of our populations. Social intelligence helps us to gauge the extent to which we are enlightened in our choices of goals and priorities, so that we strengthen our focuses on increasing the common good or social justice.

When we examine particular values that we would like to express in future societies—values such as equality, inclusiveness, diversity, cooperation, and openness—we get more direct information about present cultural trends. We also need to ask others about their views on the salience of these new values, so that we can plan to work cooperatively with them toward socially intelligent goals.

Realistically, however, it takes a critical mass of thinking individuals and groups to act collectively before our complex and powerful societies can change directions in thinking, value choices, and actions. Nevertheless, cultural enlightenment comes from many sources, so as long as we are open to new possibilities, deliberately changing our values and cultures is possible.

Social intelligence guides us to make increasingly deliberate value choices, and to review and revise our value choices where needed. When we use social intelligence we are more critical of connections that flow between our value choices and our actions, and we make adjustments to our value choices when the results of our actions are not sound or not what we expected.

It is only when our value choices and our valued ideals and goals are congruent that we act with as much social intelligence as possible. Although everyone has some social intelligence, we must be aware of our own social intelligence if we are to be effective in our societies. Furthermore, we need to make continuous attempts to increase our social intelligence, so that we can accomplish complex and daunting tasks like changing our societies' cultures in globalization.

Constructive Social Changes

Whether or not we choose to make constructive social changes in our complex societies depends in large part on our value choices. Social intelligence makes us more aware of this fact, and guides us with useful principles to reconsider our usual value choices when they do not serve our goals. In many circumstances, globalization increases complexities in our value choices, because of the growing diversity of values in each society. However, globalization in no way restricts the power of the particular value choices we make, whatever societies we live in. For example, we all continue to be faced with the existential dilemma that we can choose to orient our actions toward achieving an improved future in our societies, or we can choose to sustain injustices by maintaining our societies' status quos.

The distinctions we make in our value choices, which govern how we act now—that is, whether we try to be constructive or destructive in our accomplishments—in large part flow for our world views, and the values that sustain our world views. How we see ourselves and others prompts us to act constructively or destructively in our societies. Thus our assessments of the social consequences of our actions flow from our basic understanding of ourselves and the world—

perspectives we absorb from others, which do not become our own until we realize how we view and judge the social realities and influences in our particular situations.

When we live in times of rapid globalization, our societies often shift their priorities and allegiances. For example, rather than focus on internal matters as their highest priority, political and business leaders may attend to international dynamics and international concerns as important issues. At the same time, other societies' cultural influences infiltrate our own societies' traditional values, so that we are dazzled and distracted by multiple options for value choices. However, although we may realize that the external world affects social conditions within our societies, we sometimes become paralyzed by the influx of other societies' values, especially if there are international political tensions or wars between different countries.

Social intelligence helps us to asses these ever changing aspects of globalization by guiding us to address the impacts of the five major social influences of families, beliefs, social classes, cultures, and societies within and among societies. When we focus on how these social influences interact, we understand how social issues and social problems flow from the balance or imbalance of families, beliefs, social classes, cultures, and societies. Furthermore, considering what the common good and social justice are in particular situations allows us to use our social intelligence to make constructive social changes to benefit all.

Although establishing balance among families, beliefs, social classes, cultures, and societies yields basic conditions that allow populations to survive, by bringing about wider fulfillment in societies, we must address ongoing social issues that revolve around the major social influences of families, beliefs, social classes, or cultures. For example, when we understand the interdependence among our families, beliefs, social classes, and cultures, social intelligence principles will guide us to take specific social actions depending on which of the five major social influences needs our attention the most.

Social intelligence uses broad social perspectives to assess which value choices will accomplish our most meaningful goals. For example, which members of our populations suffer the most because of the destructive effects of families, beliefs, social classes, cultures, or societies? Which priorities do we need to establish in order to take care of personal needs as well as widespread social or international needs? What are the main characteristics of constructive social changes, given the particular facts of our social situations and global social realities?

When we use broad economic, political, cultural, and social perspectives of globalization to make these crucial decisions about our participation in constructive social changes, we do not succumb to the confusion that flows from trying to understand only fragmented impacts of globalization. Focusing on families, beliefs, social classes, cultures, and societies in globalization clarifies what our concerns need to be. Consequently, we use social intelligence principles to guide practical strategies, so that we increase the common good and social justice according to values of equality, inclusiveness, diversity, cooperation, and openness.

Social Justice

Making constructive social changes in globalization moves us toward accomplishing social justice. However, the goals of social justice, especially from the points of view of globalization, are more comprehensive than the constructive social changes that can be made in the interactions of individuals, families, communities, cultures, and societies. For example, social justice suggests allegiances to particular ideals that transcend the consequences of constructive social changes. Achieving social justice ultimately depends on accomplishing goals that honor the values and value choices of equality, inclusiveness, diversity, cooperation, and openness.

Our shared experiences of globalization are at first startling, because merely finding our bearings within globalization yields new ways to see complex international trends that we had previously tended to ignore, perhaps largely because we did not think they affected our destinies. Now that we have to acknowledge the social realities of globalization, however, we understand globalization differently, depending on whether we are from rich or poor societies.

For example, when we live in wealthy countries, we may see more easily how social class differences transcend national boundaries. Consequently, we think about countries with similar levels of economic or political development as members of similarly ranked social classes. For example, we assume social class positions that suggest special strengths or weaknesses with regard to national and international economic or political resources.

Our ideas of what social justice is are informed by our shared realizations that there are inequities throughout the world, and that these inequities are essentially unfair because they depend largely on accidents of birth. Furthermore, when we realize the extent to which populations experience inequalities within and among themselves, we often begin to consider what more just situations would be like.

Even though social intelligence does not work with mechanistic principles and formulas, there is some agreement that incorporating values and value choices in populations along lines of equality increases social justice in most problematic situations. Other values and value choices that are related to changing inequalities toward social justice include emphases on inclusiveness, diversity, cooperation, and openness.

Globalization shows us many different ways of being unequal, such as having markedly fewer opportunities to be well-educated. Social intelligence helps us to make empathic connections to societies with economic or political weaknesses and problematic educational facilities. Lacks of adequate education in these societies often affect the life chances of people with the fewest resources, so that many lives are restricted and much-needed talents are wasted. These social conditions weaken the overall strength of societies with large proportions of uneducated individuals and groups.

Social intelligence helps us to see and understand inequalities in global contexts. Although it is usually difficult to amass sufficient economic or political resources to combat these problems directly or effectively, we try to move in directions that define collective responsibilities for the well-being of populations more disadvantaged than our own.

When we take socially intelligent actions, equality for all becomes a tenable goal, and social intelligence increases our appreciation of the fact that what we do makes a difference. In the long run, our national and international security in globalization depends on there being more equal and more effective distributions of resources, at global as well as national levels of social organization.

Globalization complicates our national priorities, which means that we must persist in our efforts to understand what is going on in the world today. Reading serious newspapers and well-researched magazine articles, as well as viewing or listening to reliable news reports are helpful in this endeavor. We do not need to become educated specialists in order to deepen our understanding of international affairs, but rather we must stay alert at every turn, so that we are responsible historical actors in our value choices, decision-making, and strategies.

III. Societies and Globalization

Because our brains are important aspects of our shared evolutionary and historical development, we need to consider our economic and political relations with others through time more fully. Our capacities to educate ourselves and reflect comprehensively are important evolutionary tasks and tools, which all of us can use to further the interests of social justice in the world.

Social intelligence helps us to live up to the social justice global ideal of creating better worlds for the future, so that more populations benefit from the advantages of well-established civilizations. Consequently, social justice thrives and comes to fruition in a shared ethos of strong interests in constructive social changes, so that all ultimately tend to flourish in spite of difficult social situations.

IV. Past, Present, and Future Societies

S ocial intelligence broadens our perspectives on our complex and powerful societies, and shows us how our past, present, and future societies are inextricably linked to each other. By emphasizing the importance of understanding our societies through evolution and history, for example, social intelligence gives us a strong sense of how our societies originated, and how our past experiences have been carried forward to today's societies. Considering time in these broad terms enlarges our capacities to recognize present repetitions of past behavior and social circumstances, as well as orients us to our present and future societies.

Social intelligence is a means to balance and coordinate broad social trends in evolution, history, and the future, so that they inform our current thinking and concerns about social actions, commitments, and strategies. We need to be knowledgeable about social trends in our pasts, as well as possibilities that these may be repeated in the present, when we plan for future societies. For example, to the extent that we are aware of our shared tendencies to repeat unproductive social conflicts, we are in stronger positions to avoid them in the present and future.

The power and complexities of social trends in evolution, history, and globalization are less likely to overwhelm us— as individuals, families, communities, and cultures—when we recognize their existence, as well as their possible futility with regard to achieving goals which create better societies for coming generations. Consequently, if we stay focused on social realities such as the social facts in our present situations, we are more likely to bring about constructive social changes or increase social justice.

In many respects our cultures are the most critical catalysts for achieving success in socially intelligent ventures that define new destinies by creating more just social conditions. For example, our cultures inspire commitments to learn social facts, so that we understand shared pasts and current social needs more deeply.

At the same time that we increase the common good, our shared needs are met, and we focus more effectively on fixing whatever social conditions need to be changed in the present. Thus social intelligence guides us to meet our responsibilities to increase social resources and options for all by strengthening social values—such as equality, inclusiveness, diversity, cooperation, and openness—that sustain improved futures.

Some of the differences in the power and complexities among societies in globalization result from contrasting experiences during evolution and history. For example, we are who we are—as individuals, families, communities, and cultures—due to particular resources, events, and situations. Social intelligence helps us to come to terms with our particular heritages as cultures and societies, so that we get more in charge of our present and future circumstances. The past is indisputably behind us. Although we learn how to improve the present and future by examining past evolution and history, it is not beneficial to dwell on our pasts or try to reproduce them.

In order to move productively toward unknown futures, we must make commitments to bring particular kinds of societies into being. For example, we aim to meet social needs that guarantee the well-being of all members of our powerful and complex societies, rather than perpetuate social conditions that reinforce the material advantages of only a few members of our societies.

Thus social intelligence guides us to create social conditions which allow us to coexist peacefully amidst our rapidly changing modern societies. However, we can only achieve these significant goals when we make concerted efforts to maintain high levels of social intelligence in our endeavors, such as by deliberately increasing our social intelligence at the same time that we formulate our social strategies and interventions.

Social intelligence encourages us to coordinate our past, present, and future social needs by organizing our societies differently, so that we bring better worlds into being. For example, when we deliberately use resources that meet current individual and social needs to increase the common good and social justice, we create more satisfactory social conditions for all members of societies rather than a privileged few.

From a practical point of view, we cannot afford to build societies based on prejudice and discrimination, because this ultimately leads to our own destruction. Rather, we use social intelligence to develop policies and strategies which bring constructive social conditions into being. For example, just social conditions result from value choices that express equality, inclusiveness, diversity, cooperation, and openness. These social values lead us reliably from the past and present to improved futures.

Individuals

We experience past, present, and future concerns about our societies differently, depending on current social situations in our powerful and complex societies. However, when we are familiar with historical facts about our societies, our horizons are broad and often more closely related to ongoing present social realities than when we are focused entirely on present social conditions. Social intelligence reminds us that knowing historical facts is a significant way to understand the complexities of contemporary societies.

Although many differences in individuals' world views and orientations to societies result from their family and community histories, we also make choices about our initial experiences that determine how we act and make commitments each day. Social intelligence makes us aware of our social locations in time as well as space, for example, so that we more deliberately balance and coordinate our actions meaningfully and effectively.

Our individual differences make our experiences varied and diverse. Consequently, we develop contrasting degrees of commitment to goals, even though we may agree intellectually about which particular ends need to be met to increase the common good and social justice. Although we may not wholeheartedly believe in the importance of education for improving social conditions, we may at the same time be committed to strategies to raise minimum wages throughout societies. These variations in individual beliefs and commitments often flow from the value choices we make in directing our energies toward accomplishing our most desired objectives.

Social intelligence is based on principles that apply to people living in contrasting societies, and on principles that give a consistently high priority to maintaining individual differences in values and value choices wherever possible. Social intelligence suggests that ideally, as social human beings, we need to choose our most meaningful values to orient and guide our lives. Furthermore, social intelligence guides us to achieve challenging and daunting tasks that respond to universal needs or existential concerns.

Social intelligence encourages us to be consistent in our individual value choices, rather than avoid making value choices. Even when we associate with groups of likeminded others, in order to engage in collective actions in socially intelligent ways, we still need to preserve our autonomy as individuals. These socially intelligent considerations enable us to be more objective in choosing values that we really want to direct our actions.

We particularly need to preserve our individual autonomy when dealing with daunting circumstances, which include coping with the power and complexities of evolution, history, and globalization. According to social intelligence principles, constructive social influences of the past, present, and future need individuals' enlightened actions in order to adapt effectively to the past in the present, for better futures.

Becoming more aware of evolution, history, and globalization enables us to be responsible historical actors who scrutinize the past, present, and future to produce better worlds for more people. We must live as fully as possible if we are to create sufficient social conditions for peaceful coexistence throughout the world.

We become more socially intelligent by examining our individual histories from the points of view of our past, present, and future societies. Knowing these connections reinforces our individual worth, and helps us to recognize how we can make sound individual contributions to the common good and social justice, especially by committing ourselves to act cooperatively with likeminded others.

Although we often work with others collectively, social intelligence emphasizes the principle that we must continue to be individuals who strive to act with integrity at all times. For example, when we relate to past, present, and future societies in defining ourselves and our social missions, we are more likely to express our individual freedom and integrity through decisions, commitments, and actions.

Social intelligence is in part produced by creative societal tensions between our individualities and our needs to be integral parts of the complex and powerful societies to which we belong. Ideally, considering our relatedness to past, present, and future societies increases the flexibility of our most meaningful bonds with others, and allows us to focus on our families, communities, and cultures by assessing our actions today for tomorrow. Although we act only in the present, we choose to stay connected to our past and future societies through deciding what is best to accomplish now.

Families

Our families are tied to ancestors from the past, as well as rooted in current social situations, whether we acknowledge this or not. Furthermore, we tend to face the future more squarely through our families, because of ongoing concerns about recently born or unborn children in coming generations. Families are also very significant social groups in their own right, because traditions and societies define family memberships through blood relations or legal contracts. For example, most societies expect family memberships to last for our lifetimes—a social fact which makes family roots deep and sometimes painful.

Being individuals is closely associated with our particular family experiences, especially because most people are raised in families rather than other social groups. We first learn what interdependence and family unity are all about through our family experiences, even though we may feel completely overwhelmed by family togetherness or parental unity when we are young. For example, we realize the power of the united front of our parents—which sometimes threatens or overrides our individual wishes—as well as how our families relate to the wider worlds of communities, cultures, and societies.

One of the many contributions our families make to the development of our social intelligence is their particular orientations to past, present, and future societies. This is important because we cannot escape the impacts that our

IV. Past, Present, and Future Societies

relatives' views of past, present, and future societies have on how we consider ourselves and the world, as well as on how we assess the significance of past, present, and future time. Our understanding of evolution, history, and future possibilities is conditioned by our families' perspectives on life, especially our thinking about taking action on behalf of ourselves and others.

Traditional families tend to cling to their ancestral ties or to their roots in the past, rather than relate directly to present circumstances. The backward looking attitudes of traditional families often preserve the past, but these are usually ineffective adaptations to the present and future. Because we cannot repeat our pasts, we benefit from relating to social facts of the past without focusing solely on the past.

Families who are preoccupied with the present tend to identify themselves as modern families. However, these family members sometimes engage in risky behaviors which may lead to the demise of their families, such as separations, divorces, or geographical relocations. Unless families which try to live entirely in the present activate some meaningful connections to the past or future, their foundations are generally not sufficiently stable to endure through time.

Immigrant families, who often conduct themselves so that their children have better lives in the future, frequently sever their roots with the past, as well as deny important social realities of the present. By contrast social intelligence shows us that we are stronger as individuals, and increase our possibilities to achieve improved lives in the future, when we look to the past and present for inspiration in our daily actions as well as to the future. For example, we usually learn much about our past from past experiences in our original home countries. Furthermore, we benefit from keeping these historical facts in perspective with the present, so that we create successful futures for ourselves and our children.

Social intelligence helps us to see and understand these important variations in families' experiences of past, present, and future conditions in societies. Even if we have not had immigrant experiences ourselves, we may find similar patterns of behavior in our families, such as parents' intense desires for their children's success rather than their own fulfillment. Therefore, we need to use social intelligence to balance and coordinate the different time perspectives of past, present, and future societies, especially when trying to understand the significance of evolution, history, and globalization in our everyday lives. Ultimately, our families' orientations to past, present, and future societies are entwined with concerns about families' and individuals' survival. Thus social intelligence shows us that both our survival and fulfillment depend on family and community connections, as well as on value choices.

Because our families play crucial roles in determining how we develop as children, and which values we absorb from our relatives, patterns of emotional interdependence in our families either free or limit us in claiming our autonomy as socially intelligent actors. Furthermore, to a certain extent the power and complexities of our societies are perpetuated by emotional dynamics which resemble those in our families. Consequently, we must be prepared to struggle continuously for our autonomy in both our families and societies.

Communities

Communities essentially mediate between our families and our societies, and express qualities of life found in different parts of our societies. In part the bridging accomplished by our communities, families, and societies is often due to sharing cultural values in particular historical times, as well as making similar value choices.

For example, we benefit from learning about the outside world when our families teach us what they know about our local communities. This knowledge gives us foundations of know-how for interpreting and absorbing community experiences and world views. Our views of communities often derive mainly from our family members' understanding of our communities' dynamics. However, we may find later— as adults—that our family members' views of communities contrast starkly with others' attitudes and actions.

Communities often aim to meet some of the ongoing day-to-day needs of individuals and families. Because these basic needs are rooted in the present, communities need to be grounded in current social realities in order to be effective. However, trends in the widespread breakdown of local communities in modern industrial societies during the twentieth century are problematic, due to the fact that neither modern families nor contemporary cities support individuals and families as effectively as communities of the past. Similarly, communities which are primarily oriented toward improving our futures often do not focus sufficiently on the ongoing vital needs of individuals and families.

Social intelligence educates us about these inadequacies and weaknesses in our current communities. Although we may aspire to make concerted efforts to rebuild our communities, we need to recognize that our new designs should remake communities today rather than recreate past communities.

For example, the hierarchical social class bases of past communities reflect social class differences, rather than aim to meet community members' real individual and social needs. By contrast, today's communities are best guided by socially intelligent values such as equality, inclusiveness, diversity, cooperation, and openness, in order to produce social conditions that increase the common good and social justice.

When we deliberately build communities with social conditions that support the common good and social justice, we create microcosms of what we want our complex and powerful societies to be. Communities support our societies as well as individuals and families, for example, and it is in everyone's best interests to live in communities that are based on social values that strengthen and enrich individuals, families, cultures, and societies. These strategies enhance our efforts to increase the common good and social justice, especially when they are used in collective efforts with other members of our societies.

Social intelligence suggests that we are more likely to identify and understand particular purposes and directions for our communities when we assess social conditions within our communities in relation to our past, present, and future societies. We cannot use short term frames of reference, for example, to build lasting communities which make qualitative differences in the relatedness of individuals, families, cultures, and societies.

Because social intelligence encompasses broad perspectives related to both time and place, we consider communities with regard to past, present, and future societies in social evolution, history, and globalization. Whether we know it or not, we constantly build or rebuild our communities and societies through how we think and what we do each day. This means that whether we perpetuate or change our current thoughts and actions, we have enduring impacts on existing social structures, political policies, and social movements.

When we increase our social intelligence we heighten our awareness of the complex social dynamics of communities. This improves possibilities that we will make socially intelligent commitments to increase the common good and social justice. Although we are all historical actors, who necessarily participate in social influences that affect our social structures, it is social intelligence that directs our awareness toward social actions that neutralize or even transform our present and future communities and societies.

IV. Past, Present, and Future Societies

Although the past has gone, we constantly have opportunities to use historical facts and knowledge in the present, especially to avoid undertaking unsuccessful ventures that harm the well-being of less privileged others in our communities and societies. For example, we discern what the consequences of our actions will be when we examine events that took place in the past. Thus past social problems may inspire our missions as historical actors today, and ensure that our communities and societies are constructive social influences in present and future societies, as well as globalization.

Cultures

Social values and cultures in large part define the directions of our complex and powerful societies. When we think beyond the social structures and social processes which are directly related to individuals, families, communities, and societies, we see that our cultures answer important questions about how we relate to each other as individuals, families, communities and societies. If we want to explain human kindness, for example, we scrutinize the values of our cultures, to tell us what this means amidst the power and complexities of our societies.

Although most of our social values express social ideals which are unattainable, social intelligence helps us to realize that what we do each day inevitably expresses particular values or ideals. When we aim high to accomplish almost impossible ideals, our efforts to reach beyond ourselves and our societies may transform the directions of our lives. We also select people to be our friends, intimates, or colleagues according to our value preferences, so that subsequently our shared values define these relationships and the directions we take in our social interactions.

Cultures open doors to the future as well as to the past. When we are socially intelligent, we distinguish trends in cultures that reflect lifestyles in past, present, and future societies, for example, and we take broad perspectives in time and place in order to assess the usefulness of particular social values. If, by contrast, we decide to orient our actions toward the past, however, we tend to support cultural traditions which reinforce societies' repeated ways of meeting individual and social needs. Furthermore, established traditions often dominate societies' cultural values, so that populations continue to conform to already widely accepted standards in accomplishing their societal goals.

Social intelligence is a social value which enlightens us as well as directs our endeavors. Because social intelligence is a cultural value, we need to learn what social intelligence is, as well as increase our social intelligence. Social intelligence is not innate in substance, even though we have innate flexible capacities to be socially intelligent that protect us and help us to develop and grow. Rather, the meanings we incorporate as social intelligence are products of families, cultures, and societies that flow from our cultural and social circumstances or experiences.

Formal education derives from our cultures, and provides us with different ways to interpret the social facts of our lives and societies. We understand our particular social conditions according to characteristics of past, present, and future societies, for example, with the result that our interpretations of social situations are strongly influenced by cultural values. Thus, at least to some extent, we may be imprisoned by our cultures, because it is extremely difficult to transcend our established cultural ways of seeing and acting in varied situations.

One goal of social intelligence is to question cultural and social realities sufficiently to develop fresh ways to understand our communities and societies. New cultural values— such as equality, inclusiveness, diversity, cooperation, and openness—are substituted for more traditional, hierarchical values like social classes, for example, so that the new perspectives influence our interpretations and thinking about our commitments and actions. Consequently, when we want to innovate and make considerable changes in our lives, we choose cultural values to inspire and direct us.

Social intelligence not only points out the power of social values, but also draws our attention to the significance of particular value choices. Rather than merely absorb and use our families' values, for example, we need to be independent and deliberate in our value choices, so that we have more direct impacts on what our current and future societies are and will be. We are also more judicious in our value choices, when we know which values we want to guide our decisions and preferences.

Social intelligence shows us that when we act collectively, we predictably enhance the power of our value choices. If we act alone, although this is appropriate in particular circumstances, it is usually insufficient to bring about widespread cultural and social changes. Therefore, we need to be aware of others' values as well as our own. This helps us to unite meaningfully with likeminded others, so that we work together cooperatively to accomplish social changes that improve the quality of life for all populations in globalization.

The time frames of past, present, and future societies are important because they suggest particular value choices. When we are socially intelligent, whatever we focus on and include in our goals are value choices we make to express our social intelligence. Thus, we do not merely define what past, present, and future societies are, but we value past societies, present societies, or future societies in particular ways. Becoming socially intelligent helps us to be more objective in our value choices, so that when we see the greater good in social justice, we concentrate on what it is that we want to accomplish with regard to strengthening particular social values such as equality.

Constructive Social Changes

Social intelligence values and principles guide us to make long range constructive social changes in our communities and societies. One of the characteristics of social intelligence is that we see the broader pictures of our lives. Furthermore, we act according to these comprehensive time frames, which include considering critical dimensions of past, present, and future societies. For example, we try to be objective about the degrees of constructiveness or destructiveness of past, present, and future societies. We assess the power and complexities of the five major social influences of families, beliefs, social classes, cultures, and societies by contrasting benefits and disadvantages in past, present, and future societies.

In order to be effective in making constructive social changes in our current societies we make evolutionary, historical, and global comparisons of societies to determine which social structures and processes are best for the survival and fulfillment of all members of current societies. Is it possible to change the social organization of a particular society, for example, so that unjust social class contrasts are minimized? How can we focus on mass education facilities, so that all members of a given population receive adequate resources and attention?

When making these assessments, we need to predict what we think the social consequences will be if we maintain the status quo, and merely reinforce some of the many inequalities that exist in a particular society. For example, does it really matter if inequalities exist for certain groups in societies? Can we justify inequalities because they seem to have been necessary for supporting the smooth working of capitalism and world market economies?

The issue of making constructive social changes in the context of our past, present, and future societies is unavoidably challenging. We call into question all our assumptions about human nature and social conditions when we make decisions to impact the structures and processes of our societies. Furthermore, although social intelligence guides us when we are committed to the ideal of making constructive social changes, we also need to depend on our own initiatives and cooperation with others in order to achieve constructive social change goals through using social intelligence principles.

Social intelligence helps us in many ways. It increases our awareness of the social conditions we need to examine in making constructive social changes. It assists us in assessing the opposition we predictably face when we express our individual and collective socially intelligent initiatives. It guides our considerations of strategic options, so that we make value choices which increase the common good and social justice. And it enables us to recognize the significance of selecting the values of equality, inclusiveness, diversity, cooperation, or openness as qualities for the new social conditions we bring into being through our constructive social changes.

Past societies provide us with many examples of failed endeavors to address the needs of whole populations. In our earliest societies populations did not aim to meet the needs of all their members, but rather succumbed to the individual and social pressures of elites. It is only when our social awareness increases through time that we realize that societies thrive better when everyone's needs are addressed and fulfilled at least to some extent.

Our present societies give us many opportunities to make ongoing constructive social changes. We use past societies to learn and clarify what we want to accomplish in our present societies, so that we are more effective in selecting strategies that work well in reorganizing our populations to yield opportunities for all. We benefit from the social intelligence principle that we need to cooperate with others to achieve our goals in the long run, so we identify constructive social change opportunities by combining our visions of future societies with achieving a greater common good and social justice.

Although future societies do not yet exist, social intelligence shows us that we must lay structural foundations for communities and societies that yield possibilities for all members of populations to live fully in the future. Social intelligence shows us that one of our strongest motivations may be to work for the future well-being of our families, communities, and societies. For example, social intelligence and education show us that constructive social changes are possible, so that we become more discriminating in designing strategies and tactics to accomplish these goals.

Social Justice

Because human beings are social, we must make choices among the many different ways to conduct ourselves, get organized, and meet populations' needs. With all the good will in the world people will never be fully in charge of their destinies, so each person must continuously establish priorities and make major decisions. However, as we learn how to build more just civilizations, each generation has opportunities to choose to construct improved social conditions for all members of their populations.

Social intelligence is part of the social wisdom passed down through the ages. It is also a body of knowledge that derives from established fields of study about individuals and societies, as well as from our lived individual and social experiences. For example, social intelligence helps us to distill cultural ideas about social characteristics of individuals, families, communities, and societies in past, present, and future societies.

Social intelligence suggests that we may prevent individuals, communities, and societies from destroying each other more by supporting them than by restricting or harming them. When social arrangements are more just, individuals or groups have more adequate resources, so that the probability that present and future societies will coexist increases. For example, social intelligence and social justice help populations to be stronger and more fulfilled.

Social intelligence gives us important social know-how, and shows us that we need to focus on establishing greater equality throughout our societies in order to make the most adequate use of our resources. Although societies of the past and present have not made much progress in establishing similar opportunities for all members of their populations, the ideal of social justice is a beneficial guide in our ongoing private and public lives. When we make cooperative, concerted efforts to increase opportunities for the good life among whole populations, for example, we move in directions that increase the common good and social justice.

Social intelligence encourages us to increase social justice, but suggests that we need not work for equality in populations for moral reasons as much as for practical reasons. Although social intelligence acknowledges that we make significant moral choices every day, it emphasizes more strongly the practical necessity of taking constructive social action to minimize social inequalities, because this preserves the safety and security of societies' populations. For example, when inequalities are blatant, arbitrary, and unjust, unrest and destructive behavior predictably increase. Similarly, when considerable alienation is experienced in societies, probabilities for crime and violence increase. Furthermore, these negative trends cannot decrease until changes are made to resolve basic unjust social conditions in these societies.

Although all societies change and adapt, in order to survive in their ongoing gradual evolution, their changes must ultimately be constructive and in directions of social justice if the optimal development of populations and societies is to be achieved. Societies of the past have waxed and waned in their abilities to thrive, which shows us that no particular social changes last for ever unless we are vigilant about our ongoing value choices.

Similarly, modern societies in globalization experience various rates of change and differences in their qualities of social change. Given these social realities, we are more effective historical actors when we stay focused on social justice ideals, and use social intelligence to achieve goals that increase the common good. These are the most helpful and most hopeful directions we can take to assure that our present and future societies have open opportunities and uphold social justice values.

In many respects we need to maintain our focus on social justice ideals whatever we want to accomplish, so that we at least face in directions that will gradually accomplish these goals in the long run. For example, by educating the masses in more and more societies, we make our social justice objectives international rather than national, so that we create the peaceful coexistence necessary for meaningful rather than restrictive globalization processes. Even if we may not deliberately choose to make broad social policies to establish or confirm social justice values, we can educate others about the benefits that flow from value choices that establish equality, inclusiveness, diversity, cooperation, and openness in our present and future societies.

In order to improve our present and future societies, we go beyond maintaining the status quo or competing for upward social mobility. For example, we use our creative talents to design and construct new societies, rather than to make ever larger profits from consumer goods in our capitalist societies. Consequently, our cultures inspire

IV. Past, Present, and Future Societies

socially intelligent initiatives, because we consider social ideals from our past and present societies, and we bring new ways of interacting into being that establish social justice in our present and future societies.

V. Better Societies

If we want to reach points of agreement with others—which are usually vital preconditions for effective collective action—it is socially intelligent to agree on shared goals to create better societies today and tomorrow. Because these social processes are negotiations, which include negotiations of values, aiming to create better societies does not compromise substance, but rather becomes a strategic starting point for accomplishing specific goals.

Because "better societies" means different things to different people, social intelligence guides us to identify some of the common denominators in the assumptions we habitually make about improving our societies. For example, focusing on making constructive social changes suggests socially intelligent expediency in arriving at better societies, without defining what better societies are. Similarly, orienting our actions toward social justice suggests changes in broad ranges of substance and values about social inequalities, without much clarity about what better societies look like.

In some respects, considering what better societies are leads us to the practical socially intelligent view that even slight improvements in patterns of interactions in our current societies will create better societies. Whereas we might make deliberate use of the social ideal of social justice, to inspire our day-to-day exchanges with others, it is not actually achieving social justice that is our only goal. For example, we may more realistically aim to do better in creating social mechanisms to benefit most people in societies, thereby creating better societies in the spirit of social justice.

Societies and Social Intelligence

Social intelligence requires us to participate directly in social processes that bring about better societies for all, usually in a broad sense rather than focusing on achieving social justice in narrowly specific terms. The incremental changes implied by "better societies" means that we need not strive to meet impossible ideals, or harbor intense beliefs about overturning traditional social orders. Rather we consistently make deliberate changes to respond constructively to others' social needs, which gradually impacts social orders sufficiently to benefit all members of societies.

Actions undertaken expressly to honor those who are the least privileged among us strengthen the cores of modern, complex societies. We cannot tilt global economies to maximize profits for the wealthy, and at the same time attend sufficiently to those who are needy. The ever increasing gaps between the wealthy and the poor in prosperous industrial societies, as well as poor agricultural societies, are constant reminders that much needs to be done to reduce social inequalities, albeit in incremental ways for practical purposes.

Examining how individuals, families, communities, cultures, constructive social changes, and social justice make gradual improvements in societies shows us how social intelligence creates better societies. In addition, scrutinizing the social influences of families, beliefs, social classes, cultures, and societies helps us to understand the power and complexities of societies and social realities. Consequently, we realize that the objectivity we gain from being socially intelligent broadens our horizons, and makes our value choices more congruent with the social justice ideals of equality, inclusiveness, diversity, cooperation, and openness.

Thus social intelligence is a beacon which calls forth the individual and collective wills necessary to accomplish small or large constructive social changes in our societies.

V. Better Societies

For example, when a critical mass of individuals tries to change social class structures, new designs for social well-being predictably emerge, and our societies become more just. It is not so much that social intelligence honors only incremental social changes in producing improved societies, but rather that we need all members of our populations to participate in bettering our societies, so that collectively we get closer to expressing social justice ideals in our current and future societies.

When we examine evolutionary stages of our societies' development, historical shifts, or globalization we can identify markers of human progress, whereby social needs have been increasingly met. For example, we see how whole families, communities, and societies benefit from widespread education in some societies, so that formerly impoverished populations are more fulfilled. Social intelligence considers this progress and fulfillment to be a necessary step forward for all modern societies, so that members of the international community are more able to neutralize or minimize persisting political tensions and warfare in globalization.

Although social intelligence may not stop wars directly, becoming more socially intelligent in strategic diplomatic moves seems to be crucial for human and social survival. For example, we must be able to consider ourselves from the points of view of others' positions, including our enemies' situations, if we are to survive and create better societies. We also need to get beyond meeting only our own families' needs and wasting human potential in our societies. A basic social intelligence principle is that we are interdependent social beings, who need each other in order to survive and be fulfilled.

Individuals

Both our life experiences and our capacities to think are uniquely individual. Similarly, even though we are social beings we live and die alone, and have to assume responsibilities as individuals, however many commitments we make to be or work with others. Our individuality is therefore inescapable, as well as a basic social fact of our physiological existence.

Social intelligence draws our attention to important social contexts for understanding our individuality more fully. In addition to appreciating the significance of our own individual awareness, for example, we need to recognize how much we depend on others to inform our thinking, value choices, decisions, and actions. Although we are ultimately alone in adapting to our social worlds, we must interact with others in order to survive and be fulfilled.

Thus understanding our societies necessarily begins with knowing ourselves within our societies. For example, we are who we are due to others, and social intelligence teaches us to assess the extent to which we control what we think and how we act. This is why social intelligence uses our observations of our families, beliefs, social classes, cultures, and societies to show us how we have become who we are, and to help us to decide whether we need to change the impacts of these significant social influences on our uniqueness as individuals.

We get stronger when we become more socially intelligent, and this readies us to make commitments to create better societies. However, we need energy and resources to meet our personal responsibilities before we can improve societies, even though our attempts to create better societies may relate directly to our own and our families' present and future well-being. Furthermore, we cannot help others effectively unless we are strong, as well as sufficiently mature to interact with them in thoughtful and considerate ways.

When these conditions for taking meaningful social action are in order, we use our understanding of societies to be objective and knowledgeable in assessing our societies at present, so that we can see how they could be better in the future. We recognize ranges of practical possibilities, for example, so that we make wise choices in our decisions, and combine our resources and actions with those of other people wherever feasible.

Ideally, we enter into the business of creating better societies as individuals from positions of strength and balance. We cannot afford to skew our ideas for goals, because we want to make meaningful contributions to others as well as ourselves. Social intelligence helps us to determine what we want to accomplish as individuals, because the broad perspectives of social intelligence show us how we are related to families, beliefs, social classes, cultures, and societies.

We increase our social intelligence by making more informed decisions and commitments, which enable us to be more aware historical actors. Although we are all historical actors, who participate in historical changes whether we know this or not, social intelligence helps us to be more aware and more responsible historical actors. For example, when we are socially intelligent historical actors, we realize the consequences of our actions, and we aim more deliberately at goals that increase the common good and social justice.

Social intelligence also directs us to seek out others as individuals, so that we combine our efforts to bring about more effective social changes. We create better societies both by being individuals in our own right, and by acting in concert with those who are sufficiently like-minded to share similar goals. In so doing social intelligence helps us to deal with the inevitable social tensions that exist between our individualities and our shared togetherness with others. For example, although we take collective action in order to be effective, we must at the same time focus on our own thoughts, reactions, and responses to social pressures.

Above all, we need to stay in charge of our individual capacities to work on our own goals amidst the social pressures of others in our powerful and complex societies. It is our individual value choices, within powerful social contexts, that make differences to the qualities of life in our societies. Our value choices are our starting points for social action, and we deliberately review these same value choices whenever social tensions are difficult to manage. By focusing on self in this way, we enhance our efforts to be mature individuals who choose to create better societies.

Families

Our families are our primary crucibles for understanding ourselves and our motives, when compared to other social influences in our communities and societies. We tend to express ourselves through our family cultures, for example, which have developed from broad community and societal cultures. However, because of the close association of how we interact in our families with how we act in society at large, we need to explore our goals to create better societies by first examining who we are in the context of our families.

Our individual well-being and our characteristic behaviors are inextricably related to what goes on in our families. We benefit most from being in families which have relatively open relationships, so that communications occur not only in our nuclear families of parents and children, but also among several generations of our extended kin members. When such openness characterizes overall patterns of family interactions within families, their members are freer and more confident in their contacts with individuals or groups in communities and societies.

By contrast, the most overly rigid, stuck family relationships occur in families which have relatively few open patterns of give and take among their members. Family exchanges in relatively closed families often crystallize their restricted patterns in significant relationships such as those between spouses, parent and child, and siblings. These restricted two- or three-person repeated family exchanges frequently create estrangements within nuclear and extended families, or between nuclear and extended families. Consequently, family members in relatively closed or fragmented families are not as confident to go forward with their lives in the outside world, and often have unsatisfactory relationships with individuals or groups in communities and societies.

When we consider what "better societies" are in relation to our families, many different aspects of family needs and family responsibilities come to mind. For example, family members thrive when they are all satisfactorily housed in safe environments, adequately fed, emotionally sustained, and well-educated. Social intelligence also reminds us of the importance of ongoing family needs to orient young family members to themselves, their families, and the outside world. Consequently, from the point of view of social intelligence, families are our most significant emotional foundations for developing critical assessments of who we are, what we want to do with our lives, and what our world views are.

To the extent that we are members of open families rather than closed families, we are well-prepared to deal with stressful internal family dynamics and a wide range of different relationships in our wider communities and societies. For the purpose of understanding our families in relation to our powerful and complex societies, social intelligence suggests that when our family relationships are more balanced, we will be in stronger positions to create better societies.

Social intelligence proposes that one of the first things we need to accomplish, in increasing our social intelligence, is to come to terms with interdependencies in our families by assuming our own freedom and responsibilities, in relation to our families' patterns of dependence and dominance. Meeting these goals, which are usually extremely difficult to accomplish, increases our social intelligence. Furthermore, as we persist in our efforts to take charge of what we do in our families, we gradually become more aware historical actors. For example, we gain sufficient autonomy to make effective commitments to create better societies in the present and future.

Having strong relationships in our families prepares all family members for better lives, which includes taking advantage of possibilities to increase social intelligence and make effective social justice changes. These actions frequently have contagious effects on others in our families and in varied social settings. For example, one person's attempts to strengthen self in a family, through applying social intelligence principles, often encourage other family members to do the same in the long run. Furthermore, when socially intelligent action is taken in communities as well as families, constructive collective actions increase and create better societies.

When we use social intelligence principles to become more socially intelligent, to expand the common good, or to increase social justice, we inevitably face many individual and social challenges. However, we deal best with behavior issues, or intense social pressures in our communities and societies, when we have resolved our most difficult dominance and dependency issues in our families. For example, when we have already changed our behavior with respect to our relatives, we make more effective social changes in our communities and societies.

Communities

Communities necessarily link families to societies, and create their own distinctive cultures within societies. Although communities are not as complex or as powerful as societies, societies essentially result from many overlapping communities, so that communities are integral aspects of societies. When communities are sufficiently large, however, they often take on a life of their own, or they overlap with other communities in the complex mosaic of communities within societies.

To a certain extent communities transcend individuals and families, even though individuals and families continue to be essential components of communities throughout evolution, history, and globalization. We are points of life in our family and community networks, and we interact with others in patterns of interdependence and independence. One of our existential challenges—during evolution, history, and globalization—is to maintain freedom and autonomy within our families, communities, and societies, as well as to act and work effectively with others. However, it is often difficult for us to maintain a balance between our uniqueness and others' expectations. For example, emotional tensions between individuality and social unity make it is easier to conform to what others expect us to do, rather than carve out our own specific courses of action.

When we consider the issue of what better societies suggest in relation to today's societies, we need to understand that communities are largely inseparable from particular social characteristics of their societies. Although societies do not necessarily directly reflect their constituent communities, and communities cannot represent the full richness of social diversity in their societies, there are distinct similarities between societies and their communities, especially when communities' values are closely identified with their societies' values.

When we use social intelligence to understand our communities, we assume broad social perspectives that are based on both communities and societies, so that we see more clearly how better societies derive directly from better communities. For example, we trace social values like equality, inclusiveness, diversity, cooperation, and openness in our communities, as well as the extent to which these community values are honored and enacted throughout our societies.

Social intelligence makes us more aware of community dimensions of societies, and how communities may or may not support societies. Because we live in historical times when local communities are declining in their visibility and support of societies' networks, we may decide that the principal way to construct better societies is to create better communities.

Focusing on the well-being of our communities, rather than on our societies, necessitates asking basic questions about the nature of our communities. For example, we need to assess our most vital connections between our families and our communities. Some of our questions include examining how families orient their members to their local communities, and to what extent communities meet families' needs. We also identify specific ways in which communities meet social needs or design new ways to meet social needs. How do our communities take care of their disadvantaged members? To what extent do communities create innovative ways to meet their members' needs, such as by reducing the harmful effects of social classes?

When we increase our social intelligence we predictably participate more in making constructive changes in our communities. We see this as part of expanding the common good, for which we are all responsible. Or, when our constructive changes respond to broad issues of social justice— especially through making value choices which reflect equality, inclusiveness, diversity, cooperation, and openness—we often consider ourselves as historical actors who choose to challenge the status quo of our complex and powerful societies through our communities. Therefore our communities may become our most viable connections to our societies, as well as our most practical ways to create better societies.

V. Better Societies

Although families meet many individuals' basic needs, especially their emotional needs for support and protection, families are not self sufficient as small groups in their own right. In fact, some of our most problematic families result from cutting themselves off from their communities, so that they eventually become isolated from their communities and societies.

For example, closed families often reduce or prevent exchanges with their communities. Consequently, the emotional intensity of these same closed families increases, so that their tightened interdependence fragments their family relationships. By contrast, open families interact frequently and openly with their communities, so that both family members and communities thrive from balanced flows of communications between families, communities, and societies.

Cultures

Our families, communities, and societies are essentially held together by their cultures, which inevitably overlap with each other—sometimes to considerable extents. Because our combined cultures create the ethos of our societies, our established moral standards and our most cherished values often determine the tone and substance of our social exchanges and goals. However, even our most established cultures must remain flexible if we are to survive and be fulfilled, and if we are to create better communities and societies. This is because flexibility helps our cultures to adapt to changing situations in evolution, history, and globalization.

Sometimes the social justice values of equality, inclusiveness, diversity, cooperation, and openness are already clearly evident in our cultures, or they may need to be deliberately incorporated into our cultures through socially intelligent innovations. For example, when we choose to do things differently, we must select and decide to accept new values, so that we can design innovative goals. Thus cultures are essential aspects of achieving better communities and societies. Our cultures also enable us to consider the consequences of our actions in relation to the common good or social justice, so that we can assess the qualities of our contributions to others more accurately.

In order to continue to work toward improving our communities and societies, we need to constantly refresh our cultural knowledge with current information about our communities and societies. We are more imaginative in our endeavors, for example, when we read daily newspapers, or watch daily news reports about recent political events, artistic achievements, and scientific discoveries. Having rich, constantly changing cultural inputs to our thinking keeps us in touch with ongoing momentums of change, which makes us more likely to be effective historical actors in whatever we decide to do.

Therefore, even though we are necessarily fully immersed in our lives as individuals, families, and communities, and have clear intentions to work toward increasing the common good and social justice, we may not be truly effective until we are more aware of our cultures, as well as the wide ranges of values that cultures express. In these respects we start to appreciate how cultures and value choices are core concerns for building better societies successfully.

From the broad perspectives of social intelligence, we see that cultures are movers of varied social changes. For example, cultures precipitate changes in large groups as well as small groups; cultures encourage changes among individuals, families, and communities as well as societies; and cultures return us to the value sources of our most significant individual and social changes, especially when we evaluate the directions and consequences of societal changes. Furthermore, when we are socially intelligent we periodically reassess whether the constructive changes we try to introduce to create better societies are really happening, so that we can modify our cultural techniques and strategies when we have too little evidence of our successes.

Thus our cultures are our most reliable guides for understanding our informed intentions, decision-making, and actions. Social intelligence is a particular aspect of our cultures, which makes us more aware of our responsibilities to create better worlds. The value choices of social intelligence do not merely suggest techniques and strategies, but rather point us in directions of better societies, where values such as equality, inclusiveness, diversity, cooperation, and openness are emphasized. We make our worlds better gradually by incorporating these social justice values into our collective efforts to increase the common good wherever we can in our complex evolutionary, historical, and global societies.

When our socially intelligent views of our cultures and better societies seem remote from our everyday experiences, we need to ground our everyday decisions and actions in our individual thinking and families. This also ensures that our priorities are in line with creating better societies. Our social justice values permeate whatever we do as historical actors, particularly when we make value choices about our next best tasks to accomplish.

When we develop habits of reinvigorating our efforts through contacts with fresh cultural sources, we are more effective in making our complex and powerful societies better by increasing the common good and social justice. Cultures show us ways to go, as well as provide meanings to strengthen our motivations to make our societies better.

Constructive Social Changes

We make our most constructive social changes in our societies when we try to understand and evaluate varied social conditions in our past, present, and future societies. Social intelligence encourages us to be vigilant about maintaining these views of our social origins and prospects as we go about our daily decision-making and make commitments about how we want to spend our lives. Social intelligence also emphasizes that the more we act directly in relation to historical changes in our societies, the more successful we are in our endeavors as aware and responsible historical actors.

Social intelligence shows us that our constructive social changes may be either individual and interpersonal in scope, or collective and widespread—that is, constructive social changes that include whole societies and societies in globalization. However, whatever goals we aim to accomplish, we must focus on the value choices we want to express in our strategies, in order to confirm that what we do increases our social intelligence, expands the common good, and establishes social justice.

Because our constructive social changes do not need to be especially grand or broad, we have infinite choices in how we undertake particular tasks which we think make our societies better. Furthermore, because it is usually impossible for us to accomplish what we prefer in our powerful and complex societies, we need only move toward making our chosen goals possible. Once we establish momentums to accomplish our preferred goals, it is easier to attract interested others, so that we are ultimately more effective in achieving what we set out to do.

Although social intelligence encourages us to think big, by using broad social perspectives, and by incorporating social ideals that motivate us to increase the common good, social intelligence also points out important practical necessities. For example, we need to be realistic in our endeavors by scaling down our expectations to make constructive social changes, so that we are not too idealistic or too radical. We must see the glories that could come into being in our present and future societies, and at the same time remain sufficiently pragmatic to access particular means to accomplish our goals.

V. Better Societies

Social intelligence shows us that responsible constructive actions include intervening with moderation, as well as embracing concerns about the real consequences of our actions. We succeed in making constructive social changes when we focus our efforts on the present, for example, especially when we have already informed our current goals with historical know-how from the experiences of past societies. Our better future societies are assured when we take cues from past and present societies in order to accomplish moderate goals for constructive social changes now.

When we realize the importance of having some degree of social acceptance for our socially intelligent innovative changes, we deliberately use cultural resources to establish meaningful contacts with other people. We cannot afford to act in a cultural vacuum, or to focus too closely on our individually-oriented social contributions. We need to work with like-minded others as much as possible, in order to make constructive social changes happen, as well as to reach those who accept the socially constructive changes we designed.

Social intelligence draws our attention to the fact that the outreach of our social actions is significant for better present and future societies only when our strategies are constructive. For example, in hierarchically organized societies we need to be sure that we base our actions on social justice values such as equality, inclusiveness, diversity, cooperation, and openness. Moreover, we stay on course with our good intentions for making constructive social changes in social classes by continuing to increase our social intelligence.

We ensure that we are actually expanding the common good, by periodically checking whether or not working towards classless societies is central in our plans and actions. Often, we succeed in accomplishing this only by making our goals to meet the needs of disadvantaged individuals, or less privileged groups, our highest priority. In this way, our actions are socially intelligent and strategic for designing and implementing alternatives to hierarchical social classes in our present and future better societies.

Social intelligence suggests that making constructive social changes is necessary for our shared survival and fulfillment. We cannot fool ourselves indefinitely that what we do does not matter, or that societies can continue to foster their special interests with complete disregard for the needs of all. Rather we must find ways to awaken our individual and social responsibilities to be good caretakers of the best we have in our civilizations, as well as to create new and better societies.

Social Justice

One way to create better societies is to focus on social justice. For example, we consider how societies have become more just through time—by examining evolutionary, historical, and global evidence of social justice in different societies—so that we become more committed to further social justice in our present and future societies.

Focusing on social intelligence makes us realize that social facts from evolutionary, historical, and global societies suggest that gradual progressions toward social justice are possible. Consequently, when we understand social realities in our societies more fully—especially how the five major social influences of families, beliefs, social classes, cultures, and societies may often take over our lives when we do not pay sufficient attention to our value choices and priorities—we are more inclined to assume both overall and specific responsibilities to work toward achieving social justice for all.

Learning about social intelligence and increasing our social intelligence, through both our individual and collective efforts, often leads us to work toward goals that accomplish social justice. We may gradually become aware of compelling reasons to establish social justice for all, for example. We realize that we cannot spend our lives merely satisfying our own self-interests, or perpetuating social inequalities that hurt many people, including entire populations.

We become pragmatists because we realize that our true prosperity depends on meeting our own and others' needs, rather than on ignoring or limiting others' opportunities to live fully. We act toward the particular goals of social justice not only because they reflect moral or ethical principles, but because we and our densely peopled planet will not survive unless we do so.

Focusing on concerns to establish better societies enables us to see that only when we orient our actions toward social justice can we hope to create social conditions that promote peaceful coexistence. When we inadvertently perpetuate the status quo, we not only prolong and exacerbate social problems related to social inequalities, but we enlarge gaps between opportunities for the rich and poor to live fully within and among populations through time. Therefore, deliberately choosing social justice values like equality, inclusiveness, diversity, cooperation, and openness becomes a necessary condition for achieving peaceful coexistence.

In modern societies we usually survive by reacting to the push and pull of social trends, rather than by acting in relation to well-considered goals. For example, we are easily overwhelmed by anxieties that surface due to virtually unrecognized social conditions in our lives. Consequently, many aspects of being alive that we care for the most seem to be out of our grasp or out of control. However, social intelligence educates us about value options which strengthen our resistance to secular or consumer pressures on our everyday lives.

Social intelligence gives us reasons to live when we cannot find any, as well as meanings and purposes to follow when we are trapped in our daily routines. One of the most valuable dividends of increasing our social intelligence is that we discover more freedom and authenticity in our daily choices, and our everyday intentions get more directly connected to creating better worlds.

Merely having an interest in constructing better social conditions is a sufficient purpose to motivate us to get on with our lives, so that we make more meaningful contributions to others. This new direction helps us to commit ourselves to engage in actions which increase social justice, so that we save ourselves as well as others. Working toward social justice rescues us from alienating social conditions like social inequalities, isolation, meaninglessness, normlessness, powerlessness, and self-estrangement, because we focus on replacement social values like equality, inclusiveness, diversity, cooperation, and openness. Constructive social conditions improve the lives of all, and break down some of the artificial distinctions made by omnipresent, relentless social classes in modern societies.

Social intelligence makes our tasks to create better societies for all less daunting. When we use social intelligence, and pursue goals based on social intelligence principles, we gain sufficient vision to tackle specific aspects of social injustices in our societies. Instead of being afraid to move in directions which establish social justice directly, we take courage from actualizing possibilities to create better societies, especially when we see some evidence of our successes in everyday situations.

The rewards of accomplishing socially intelligent actions increase social justice and encourage us to continue in these directions. We grow wiser in our efforts, and more enlightened in our understanding of ourselves and our societies. Even though these dividends may not be immediately tangible, they are bases for strong socially intelligent hopes about better futures, wiser future generations, and new traditions of social justice.

Social Intelligence and Societies

VI. Social Intelligence Perspectives

The know-how of social intelligence derives from broad perspectives on social realities, individuals, and societies. Although each person is a self, social intelligence considers us as actors in powerful social contexts that stretch beyond our individual decisions. As well as being unique separate human beings, social intelligence reminds us that we are members of the human race in evolution. Also, our shared histories from the dawn of civilizations make us current agents of change in contemporary historic times.

Social intelligence applies to a broad and deep range of different social concerns. For example, social intelligence principles are based on the social fact that we are integral parts of complex and powerful social realities and collective lives. We belong to an historic present and past, but at the same time our decisions control our lives to some extent. Although our present options may sometimes seem clear, we are often baffled in recognizing what it is that we should do next, and what we need to do in order to live fully.

Social intelligence guides us whether we think we know which way to go, or whether we stay still—sometimes paralyzed—in confusion. Social intelligence makes us aware that we have choices in how we understand our worlds, as well as in how we act and commit ourselves to specific present or future directions. For example, our pasts may suggest current directions for our decisions, or we may take risks by choosing to go in new directions.

We benefit from the central socially intelligent idea that life is broad, with many possibilities, which increases the likelihood that we will move forward by seizing socially intelligent opportunities. By contrast, when we choose to remain stationary, by spinning our wheels in daily routines, we gradually deplete our vital life energies without accomplishing our preferred goals.

If we get too caught up in limited trajectories, we are gradually overwhelmed and absorbed by the power and complexities of our societies. By contrast, to the extent that we keep our individual and social uniqueness strong, especially by acting to accomplish meaningful goals with like-minded others, we increase both our own and others' fulfillment as we create better societies.

Social intelligence shows us that existentially all populations share some similar life circumstances. For example, we need to assume responsibilities that help us to survive and lead meaningful lives. Thus, we try to think clearly and independently in order to know what the next best thing is for us to do, as well as meet our shared needs. Social intelligence teaches us how to think and weigh our options, which at the same time clears our minds of destructive thoughts that defeat our best purposes.

Principles of social intelligence guide our actions as well as clear our minds. We learn how to make our best efforts when we move toward increasing social justice, for example, because we find opportunities to work with like-minded others, as well as actively pursue our most viable dreams for better societies. Social intelligence also helps us to recognize significant social influences in evolution, history, and globalization, so that we coordinate our knowledge of social needs in relation to past, present, and future societies.

In many vital respects social intelligence is synonymous with enlightenment, and includes assuming responsibilities such as increasing the awareness of others, especially by working together to accomplish social justice. Social intelligence principles help us to set world changes in motion, even though we know that some of our goals cannot be achieved in our lifetimes. By actively trying to meet the needs of all members of our populations, we turn our backs on maintaining the status quo, and on making it possible for different elites to continue to have power and control over the lives of less advantaged people.

Social intelligence encourages us to create better societies, where all are sufficiently free to enjoy privileges that historically were restricted to members of upper social classes. By participating in democratic social actions, social intelligence opens doors for all, and improves the lot of those who have suffered for generations.

Although we necessarily fail to achieve some of our best intentions to accomplish social justice, we realistically aspire to have better communities and better societies when we apply socially intelligent principles in our actions. For example, choosing values that promote constructive changes in our societies influences the well-being of individuals, families, communities, cultures, and societies, especially when our coordinated actions are enlightened by social justice goals.

Close-Up Views

Social intelligence is characterized by particular ways of looking at ourselves and the world that combine taking close-up views of social realities with seeing far. We deliberately use social intelligence to see the broader pictures of our lives, for example, but at the same time make sure that we do not let go of our understanding of important social conditions in our immediate present experiences. When we use social intelligence to improve our capacities to take meaningful and effective social actions, we realize that what goes on in our personal exchanges is understood more fully from these broader viewpoints.

Socially intelligent ways to understand our social worlds become beacons of enlightenment for us and others. However, unless we apply principles of social intelligence to our everyday decisions and actions, we easily lose this grounding in immediate social realities. For example, we need to see how families, beliefs, social classes, and cultures affect us and our societies if we are to make responsible contributions to our societies.

The reason that social intelligence is so necessary for our survival and fulfillment is that it gives us sufficient freedom and know-how to make needed contributions to the common good and social justice. For example, only when we see direct connections between how we live and how societies are, are we able to create effective social changes through our everyday decisions and value choices. However, our close-up views of our lives are necessarily distorted when we allow only a near-sightedness of our personal and social realities to govern how we think about ourselves and others.

Once we recognize that our socially inadequate close-up views of daily interactions reinforce the status quo of our societies, we realize that we have options to make more authentic decisions about how to spend our limited energies. For example, we see that putting our reflections and decisions in broad social contexts increases our objectivity and effectiveness, especially in terms of achieving those goals that we really want to accomplish.

If we do not habitually make connections between our close-up views of social realities and seeing far, we inevitably lose some of our personal and social freedoms. For example, when we persist in using only our close-up views of social realities, we imagine that these make up our true worlds, instead of remembering that we are integral parts of broad social processes. Focusing only on our close-up views inevitably reduces our opportunities to be fulfilled as individuals and participants in globalization. At the same time, our close-up views magnify and distort the overall importance of our day-to-day routines.

To the extent that we continue to define our worlds narrowly, the scope of our actions is unnecessarily limited and uninspired. We cannot reach out effectively to societies when we immerse ourselves in our distorted close-up views of local social realities. Furthermore, we cannot find ultimate meanings, purposes, and directions in our immediate busyness and reactivity to others. Close-up views of ourselves and our social circumstances stop us from developing expansive trajectories that allow us to claim the freedom we have, with the result that we suffer from feeling trapped by our situations and social realities.

Social intelligence in no way requires us to deny or ignore close-up views of our lives. Although close-up views of social realities may not alert us to their destructive qualities, or to the damaging effects we may experience from past social circumstances, social intelligence continues to guide us in how to further our personal and social needs to live fully through making constructive contributions to others.

We must pay attention to our immediate circumstances, as well as to our existential yearnings for more rewarding experiences, by letting social intelligence show us how to become more active agents in both our personal and broader destinies. Thus, we follow the guidance of social intelligence to connect our close-up views of social realities with seeing far into our complex and powerful societies in globalization and evolution.

We return to our close-up views of social circumstances most purposefully when we decide on anchors for our reflections, thinking, and decision-making. These bases do not disappear or become unimportant when we get increasingly committed to expanding our social intelligence and being responsible historical actors. We merely need to return to our most immediate social anchors occasionally when we continue to examine the broad social influences of families, beliefs, social classes, and cultures in our complex and powerful societies. However, we cannot afford to get stuck in the immediacy of our present situations, because this makes us lose our effectiveness as agents who create better societies.

Close-up views tell us where our attention is focused, and how well we live up to our destinies as historical actors. For example, we have to respond to the real needs of our families, before we can successfully examine the broader outreaches of families, beliefs, social classes, cultures, and societies. We must also make sure that we no longer contribute to problematic interdependencies in our families, so that we bring our socially intelligent maturity to bear in making decisions about communities and societies. Our efforts to create better futures for our societies become more effective when they flow from our deep understanding of the immediacy and power of our current and continuing social situations.

Seeing Far

One of the most distinctive characteristics of social intelligence is that it requires us to understand our social circumstances from where we are at present in the world to the future. For example, social intelligence encourages us to learn as much as we can about the breadth of our universes, so that we see how we are related to both globalization and evolution. We are creatures of evolution, history, and globalization, who are deeply rooted in the past, present, and future.

When we secure our local bearings in order to understand the power and complexity of ourselves and our societies, social intelligence shows us that we interact with those closest to us in customary ways, and that the networks of our personal relationships, communities, and societies stretch into distant pasts as well as the far future. We essentially straddle social intersections of time and place, which create social environments for our being and life chances. Given this complexity in our ongoing social connections, social intelligence helps us to choose how to relate responsibly to our past, present, and future worlds.

The principles of social intelligence are based on experiential knowledge about our practical day-to-day challenges to survive and be fulfilled. Because we are both non-rational and rational beings, we must find ways to be rational about our non-rational inclinations, so that we are more in charge of our destinies and the destinies of our societies. As we grow and mature, we realize that we must express the power of good in the world if we are to survive and be fulfilled. Social intelligence helps us to accomplish this by heightening our social awareness, and by strengthening our individual and collective wills to accomplish goals that create optimal social conditions for all.

Socially intelligent views of social well-being require us to see and understand our global circumstances, as well as our local conditions. Cultivating sufficiently accurate perspectives about distant social realities helps us to accomplish this, and at the same time increases our social intelligence. For example, getting to know more about world history increases our responsible commitments to participate more deliberately in globalization.

Social intelligence guides us to pay particular attention to local and global patterns of behavior, which reflect the underlying non-rational or emotional significance of our families, beliefs, social classes, cultures, and societies. We get to know the global social contexts of our societies, for example, when we understand how our families, beliefs, social classes, and cultures provide us with broad ranges of value choices and behavior possibilities. The options we select ultimately sustain or diminish particular values, which create social conditions that support all members of populations or destroy societies and civilizations.

Our stakes in societies' survival and fulfillment are high. We seize personal and societal destinies which improve social conditions for all, or we perpetuate elites based on assets, power, and force which focus solely on using rich resources to achieve narrow, personal gains. Our existential dilemma is to decide whether we want to truly share the goods of our universes, or whether we prefer to amass the most resources for ourselves regardless of the plights of others.

We cannot make these value choices in socially intelligent ways unless we train ourselves to see far into the circumstances of those who live in distant places as well as in our home territories. We need to explore the social consequences of families, beliefs, social classes, cultures, and societies in globalization, for example, so that we know that we go forward with our lives toward better societies, rather than backward to uneducated or ignorant narrow concerns. Ideally, we become more responsible historical actors by seeing far. Seeing far enables us to develop broad socially intelligent perspectives, which guide us to balance local and global social realities with their different demands on our time and energy.

Whenever our current circumstances are difficult to deal with, social intelligence encourages us to take a step back from our involvement with immediate pressing issues, so that we can be more objective. For example, seeing far into different places and different times is a reliable way to cultivate the detachment needed to think clearly. Furthermore, social intelligence honors the social fact that our brains are essential for our survival in evolution, which inspires us to think more deeply about creating better societies and better worlds.

Changing Views

In some respects the different perspectives of social intelligence—families, beliefs, social classes, cultures, and societies—include a wide range of vantage points from close-up views to seeing far, and are themselves principles of social intelligence. The different perspectives of social intelligence are so important to understanding what social intelligence is, that they become critical dimensions of social intelligence.

Socially intelligent perspectives help us to understand the everyday lives of individuals, communities, and societies amidst the social changes of evolution, history, and globalization. For example, we appreciate the power and complexities of the five major social influences in societies, because they express the sum total of strongest social influences in past, present, and future societies, and serve us as significant social resources to increase the common good and social justice. These societal processes— families, beliefs, social classes, cultures, and societies—are the lifeblood of our civilizations, survival, well-being, and fulfillment.

As well as deliberately strengthening our understanding of the five major social influences of families, beliefs, social classes, cultures, and societies as different perspectives of social changes, we must be prepared to deal with the great unknowns of social changes. Human beings struggle in evolution and history, which helps them to come to terms with the power and complexities of their societies. For example, they try to ensure that no stones are left unturned in their relentless searches for truths. Given the existence of many social ambiguities, social intelligence is a truth that carries us forward to create better societies and civilizations, rather than backward and away from our social ideals.

We make commitments to take forward-looking and forward-going trajectories when we focus on increasing our social intelligence. To the extent that we harness our energies to increase our social intelligence, we increase probabilities for achieving the common good and social justice, we heighten our awareness as historical actors, and we work cooperatively with others to achieve social justice ideals like equality, inclusiveness, diversity, cooperation, and openness.

Some of the most reliable routes to accomplishing these goals include becoming as objective as possible when we choose social intelligence perspectives to guide our actions. For example, we continue to make every effort to understand the substantive power and complexities of the five major social influences of families, beliefs, social classes, cultures, and societies.

When we realize that globalization is based on changing social realities, we start to identify the complex interplay of the critical social influences of families, beliefs, social classes, cultures, and societies within evolution and history. Moreover, we heighten our awareness of past, present, and future societies, in order to be socially intelligent in making constructive differences in how we live and organize ourselves.

Changing our views of social realities is an essential aspect of using social intelligence to live productively as individuals, communities, and societies. When we are socially intelligent, for example, we deliberately move our perspectives between close-up views of interactions to seeing far, so that we remain objective, flexible, and open-minded in our assessments of our current and future social situations. We cannot depend on static ways to view our current worlds, if we are to deal successfully with contemporary social problems. Consequently, changing our views of social realities enables us to work effectively toward collective goals of increasing the common good and social justice.

Cultivating habits which change our views of social realities ensures that we stay on track as historical actors. This helps us to design constructive social changes and better societies more effectively. We also develop sufficient vision to make our lives more fulfilling when we move between and among different social intelligence perspectives. For example, we change our views of social realities in order to think through what we need to do next—individually or with others—in order to achieve more just societies.

When we become responsible historical actors, we make mature value choices which relate to different dimensions of our societies. However, we cannot increase the common good and social justice without having particular values in mind, which add meaning, purpose, and direction in our lives. We understand that whatever we do inevitably impacts others, and we see ourselves as active players in evolution, history, and globalization.

In some respects being socially intelligent is synonymous with seeking and finding our destinies as agents of vital social changes. Furthermore, we get stronger by helping others to live more fully as well as ourselves. We live up to our responsibilities, so that future as well as present generations benefit from our deeds in meaningful ways.

Major Social Influences

Social intelligence not only gives us useful perspectives on social conditions during evolution, history, and globalization—which deepen our understanding of past, present, and future societies—but also illuminates vital connections that need to be made among individuals, communities, and societies in these change processes. What is it that nurtures individual and community loyalties to our societies? What helps us to make the most constructive changes in our communities, societies, and globalization? How can we understand ourselves sufficiently to bring about constructive social changes?

One way to see how our human and social natures derive from complex and powerful influences in our societies is to single out which social influences are strongest in orienting us to ourselves, others, and future societies. How do we become more responsible actors, so that we are increasingly in charge of our destinies? How do we launch our children into societies, so that they lead productive lives which benefit others as well as themselves? What does success really mean? How can we lead our most meaningful lives, as well as act thoughtfully in meeting each challenge that comes our way?

Social intelligence answers these searching questions directly, with practical suggestions and guidance about how to make significant value choices that affect us, our families, our communities, and our societies. For example, in order to achieve sufficient personal and social maturity, we must learn about which social influences impact the qualities of our lives most deeply, and which social influences determine our everyday decisions and actions. Five major social influences which form many of our assumptions about ourselves and our social realities are our families, beliefs, social classes, cultures, and societies.

In many respects our families form the social and emotional foundations of our identities and world views. For example, our social intelligence flows from our experiences and understanding of the most intense patterns of interdependence in our families, so that in order to increase our social intelligence we must think differently and do things differently. How can we be more objective about our family dependencies, so that we free ourselves from entrapment in our most intense family dependencies? How do we both meet our family responsibilities and go forward into our communities and societies to increase the common good and social justice?

Our beliefs govern much of our thinking. For example, we take many of our strongest beliefs for granted, and experience them as "natural" or "right" when we may not have thoughtfully assessed their truths from the points of view of social realities. How can we understand the social origins of our beliefs sufficiently, so that we nurture beliefs which provide us with constructive social guidance, and let go of beliefs which are destructive for us and others?

The power and dominance of social classes in our everyday thinking is a social influence that frequently defines our assessments of social situations before we decide to act. Unless we realize the pervasiveness of our social classes at all levels of our understanding, we are unable to be objective about the many choices and possibilities we have for reorganizing our societies. For example, how necessary is it for us to compete with each other in order to gain upper class social privileges, especially when we know that this detracts from solving social issues that result from social inequalities?

Cultures are major social influences that pervade our societies. We necessarily develop allegiances to particular cultures, especially our families' cultures, in order to become human and social. We are loyal to specific values and ideals, for example, which we take for granted as significant aspects of our social realities and lived experiences. Social intelligence guides us in sorting out those cultural ties that habitually diminish our goals and objectives, so that we can free ourselves sufficiently to increase the common good and social justice.

Lastly, our complex and powerful societies create social conditions that support or limit our capacities to be effective historical actors. We may or may not receive satisfactory educations, for example, which ideally strengthen independent thinking and capacities to work cooperatively with others. Societies may also resist social changes by perpetuating rigid traditions that do not welcome modernity. Thus the power and forces of existing societies control some of the most vital choices about societies that individuals can make, which may ultimately limit equality, inclusiveness, diversity, cooperation, and openness in their populations.

Social progress is halted by societies when social inequalities are increased rather than decreased. However, social intelligence helps us to be aware of these negative tendencies, and suggests social justice as a practical ideal for guiding historical actors to make changes that increase the common good for all.

Making Sense of Our Social Worlds

Among other benefits, social intelligence helps us to make sense of our social worlds. We gain from this because increasing meaning in our lives strengthens our motivations to make contributions to others as well as our families. Although we necessarily continue to be aware of the power of our self interests, we begin to understand more fully the needs of those less fortunate than ourselves, for example, so that we make more objective assessments of what we can do to increase the common good and social justice.

Because social intelligence requires us to scrutinize our beliefs and motivations, we are more careful about choosing our preferred values to guide what we do each day. When we are deliberate in making value choices, as well as understand the social origins of our preferred values, we are more objective about ourselves, the choices we make, and the choices we could make. At the same time that our social worlds gain meaning, we become more socially intelligent and more in control of our lives, including making contributions to our communities and societies. Thus making sense of our social worlds strengthens our responsibilities as historical actors who increase the common good and social justice.

Social intelligence is knowledge that has accumulated from our lived experiences, social facts about societies, and social wisdom. When we are socially intelligent, we enlighten ourselves with facts that are rooted in social realities—such as the major social influences of families, beliefs, social classes, cultures, and societies—so that we are more pragmatic in how we act in relation to our families, communities, and societies. For example, we strengthen ourselves by becoming more autonomous in our families, with the result that we are more independent and more effective in our efforts to achieve increasingly meaningful goals.

The deeper understanding we gain from increasing our social intelligence enables us to find more meaning in our social worlds. For example, we identify patterns and repetitions in our families' interactions, which enable us to be more objective in assessing how we want to be and act in our most personal relationships. We scrutinize our beliefs so that we deliberately select and nurture our most meaningful beliefs, and let go of beliefs that hinder or discourage us in creating better worlds. We see social classes for what they are through the limits they impose on members of disadvantaged groups. Furthermore, we appreciate our cultures as sources of values, ideals, and value choices, which help us to make more sense of what we do and how we contribute to others.

As we continue to make sense of our social worlds, we find more reasons to accomplish goals that we had not considered seriously before. Also, it is through sharing similar values and goals with others that we become more effective in expressing meanings that guide us to create better futures for all.

Thus we find meaning in whatever we do if we are to be socially intelligent in our actions, and if we are to increase the common good and social justice. For example, when we consider existential issues about our survival and fulfillment, we see more clearly that we need to address the needs and yearnings of members of disadvantaged groups in order to be fulfilled ourselves.

When we are socially intelligent, we understand that ultimately our survival depends on a shared destiny that is built on the well-being of all members of societies, rather than on the accumulated resources of members of elites and upper social classes. We realize that social justice in societies increases the well-being of all, in part because social justice gives members of lower social classes the privileges of equal opportunities and meaningful lives.

The sense we make of our social worlds derives from our individual and collective efforts to do what we think is right and appropriate, given the social facts of our particular social situations. For example, we gain the most meaning and sense about our social worlds when we try to understand who we are and who we could be in relation to our social worlds.

These personal starting points orient us to the past, present, and future with social intelligence. Furthermore, having the goal of expanding our social intelligence moves us in meaningful directions, which increase the sense we make of ourselves and our social worlds. Eventually, our persistence in increasing our social intelligence renews our senses of purpose, which motivate and fuel our actions as historical actors.

Eternal Values

One of the ways in which we make sense of our most mundane daily routines is to view our behavior in relation to eternal values—that is values which transcend particular societies and particular times. Social intelligence puts us in touch with the power of values, especially those values which have persisted through long periods of time. Long-lasting values are often thought of as eternal, because they emerge and re-emerge over several historical eras. For example, social intelligence suggests directing attention to eternal values such as social justice, equality, inclusiveness, diversity, cooperation, and openness, because these particular eternal values inspire us to build better societies.

VI. Social Intelligence Perspectives

Social intelligence may also be thought of as an eternal value when we envision our futures, because it expresses ongoing human capacities to act for the good of all peoples. In these respects, social intelligence shares some of the powerful qualities of other eternal values. As well as enduring through varied times and circumstances, for example, social intelligence and other eternal values motivate individuals, families, communities, and societies to seek and implement improved ways of organizing and dealing with each other, so that peaceful co-existence and fulfillment become possible for all. In addition, social intelligence makes us aware of the power of eternal values, so that when we choose goals that express eternal values, they enhance our daily effectiveness as historical actors.

Social intelligence not only heightens our awareness of particular qualities in our shared social conditions, but also inspires us to take practical actions to improve social conditions directly related to increasing survival and fulfillment in our powerful and complex societies. For example, if we honor eternal values in secular or religious contexts, we more easily find sufficient energies to bring about constructive social changes. Eternal values, such as love and learning, move us to cultivate cooperative and open relationships with others, which strengthen and enhance our collective efforts to create better societies.

Eternal values are a significant influence on our behavior because they emanate from our cultures, especially from wide varieties of sacred and secular values. Although eternal values are often difficult to substantiate or illustrate with social facts, historical records show how different eternal values have varying impacts in different societies through time.

Our missions as socially intelligent historical actors may include strengthening the power of eternal values that are currently underestimated or unappreciated in our modern societies, such as equality. When we increase our social intelligence we find that focusing on expressing a single eternal value in our everyday actions can transform our individual lives, families, communities, and societies. These results show us the remarkable and undeniable social power of eternal values in our cultures and in our socially intelligent actions.

Eternal values help us to think more clearly because we assess our actions more objectively when we act and review our actions in relation to them. We see more possibilities and opportunities for creating constructive social changes, for example, when we allow ourselves to be guided by eternal values directly related to social intelligence and social justice. Social intelligence helps us to assume more objective postures about values and value choices, which deepens our understanding of available means to bring about significant social changes that impact the lives of all.

As individual historical actors, one of our most important socially intelligent tasks is to scrutinize and change the value choices we make in our everyday lives. When we move in directions which take us closer to expressing eternal values, for example, we often have the greatest constructive impacts on the lives of others. We learn how to put ourselves in others' social situations, so that we can make more effective moves to improve social conditions for all.

A consequence of carefully selecting eternal values to direct our actions is that we gauge the effectiveness of our contributions more carefully and more accurately. Furthermore, nurturing eternal values increases our motivations to face problematic social circumstances, because focusing on eternal values helps us to transcend the inevitable harshness of others' reactions to some of our innovative intentions and strategies.

In many respects responsibility is viewed as an indispensable eternal value. When we strive to be more responsible, or find more ways to be responsible through our actions, we are more enlightened in what we decide, what we do, and what we accomplish. For example, believing in the power of being responsible in our choices, decisions, and actions enables us to weather others' resistance to our intentions to create better societies and bring them into being.

VII. Families and Beliefs

Families are the first, most influential component of social intelligence. Because families have such powerful influences on how we see ourselves and our societies, our social intelligence necessarily derives from family experiences and family facts whether we acknowledge this or not. Furthermore, in order to increase our social intelligence, we confirm or re-establish the foundations of our social intelligence gradually, in relation to social facts expressed through repeated patterns of interactions in our families.

We are who we are largely due to the ways in which we are habitually independent or dependent in our families. Furthermore, our families are significant because they are usually the primary social sources of our beliefs. For example, when we are children, we absorb many of the most powerful values of our parents and siblings as our own, with the result that we can often only change our beliefs effectively by interacting differently in our families.

Thus both our families and our beliefs are important major social influences, which either restrict or expand our social intelligence, largely because they connect us directly to some of our deepest emotions as well as to some of our most significant relationships and social trends. For example, we tend to invest strong emotions in dependent patterns of family interaction, or in particular beliefs, with the result that we give them considerably more power over our decisions and life outcomes than if we were more objective about our options. This is why the broad perspectives of social intelligence help us to come to terms with the seemingly determining impacts of our family interactions and beliefs. This is also why our value choices, which influence our most strongly preferred goals, are usually difficult to change.

Some of the most compelling conditions in our families are their obvious and subtle pressures to conform to family members' expectations. When we are young, we are disciplined to follow in the footsteps of our parents or elders, so that in many respects it may be supremely challenging to think for ourselves, or to act independently of our relatives. For example, we absorb others' views of us and the world in order to be accepted, and in order to feel as though we belong to our families, because we need strong family bonds to survive.

Social intelligence recognizes our primary needs to survive through our families, and at the same time encourages us to examine our behavior critically. Do we replicate patterns of family behavior that are not useful in our current social situations? Do we have contradictory beliefs that cannot guide us to decide what we want to do with our lives?

Taking broad perspectives on our families, beliefs, social classes, cultures, and societies puts concerns about our families and beliefs in meaningful contexts, so that we are freer to choose which beliefs we really want to keep, and which we need to change or release. By substituting more productive patterns of behavior, or truer beliefs for beliefs which were integral parts of our initial programming, we become surer that we are living according to our own preferences. Furthermore, we use social intelligence to guide us in formulating more effective strategies to deal with our families and maintain new beliefs.

Social intelligence guides us to develop flexible patterns of interacting in our families and other social groups. This allows us to change how we respond to our relatives in ongoing interactions. Similarly, social intelligence helps us to link our beliefs to our actions more directly, so that we clarify our motives and focus on our priorities. However, even though our starting points in applying social intelligence are to understand how both our families and beliefs influence what we do, we also need to educate ourselves about the extent to which families and beliefs in societies influence our actions.

Because families and beliefs can be determining factors in our personal lives, they have strong impacts on how societies are organized, and on how they adapt to historical circumstances. We are who we are partly because of how we allow our families and beliefs to influence us, and partly because of how families and beliefs impact our societies. For example, societal views of acceptable family behavior become standards or norms that control individuals, families, communities, and societies. Similarly, current societal beliefs determine which beliefs are used and maintained by individuals, families, communities, and societies.

Social intelligence helps us to see both these interpersonal and broad social connections with families and beliefs, and helps us to control their impacts on our behavior. When we learn more about the complex societal aspects of our family dynamics, as well as the power of our societies' beliefs and social motivations, we become more independent in our negotiations with others. For example, we understand more fully how patterns of behavior tend to be repeated in societies as well as in families. Consequently, we pay more attention to major societal trends in families and beliefs, so that we are more effective in increasing the common good and social justice.

Family Foundations

When we consider social intelligence in relation to our complex and powerful societies, we acknowledge that the social sources of what we accept as human nature are often our families. For example, whether or not most people in most societies become who they are as adults through the tenacious impacts of their families' interactions, we usually accept this as a working premise in making sense of our worlds.

The power that families have over us flows from the social fact that we are deeply impressionable when we are children, as well as particularly needy. Consequently, we absorb many of the most dominant ideas and beliefs of our parents and relatives as we grow and develop. We also tend to imitate—or rebel against—what our emotionally closest relatives do in their decision-making and actions during our adolescence.

We often deny the existence of these links between our family experiences, our understanding of human nature, and our societies. For example, we may prefer to think that we automatically discard our early impressions of what life is all about, especially as we become more educated and more sophisticated through formal academic knowledge.

However, if we are sufficiently observant or socially intelligent, we can trace many of our basic inclinations about taking action to repeated patterns of dependence and interdependence in our families. These ties to our families express the most powerful emotional foundations of our being, our decisions, and our actions. They are also foundations of our complex and powerful societies, whether we like or accept this social fact or not.

When we want to be more socially intelligent in order to live more fully, or to be more effective in how we interact with others, we must see ourselves and our societies in broad perspectives which honor the special significance that families have in influencing our decisions, commitments, and life outcomes. Because we are oriented by our families to believe in certain world views, which include images and visions of societies' possibilities, we must find ways to change our world views when they block our efforts to accomplish our preferred goals. For example, if we are not successful in achieving our most cherished goals, we need to return to the original social sources of our families, in order to change our world views and strengthen our interpersonal strategies.

Social intelligence helps us to acknowledge the power of our families by highlighting the significance of our continued emotional attachments to past and ongoing patterns of family behavior as we make everyday decisions. We also learn to recognize how our families' cultures and values influence our life outcomes.

Even though most intergenerational exchanges in our families may seem to be benign and constructive, social intelligence requires us to assess our independence, freedom, and autonomy through examining our families. This is important because family interactions are a primary way to change ourselves, clarify our priorities, and increase our social intelligence.

Scrutinizing how our families impact who we are and what we do as adults has significant social consequences, which ultimately affect the well-being of entire societies and globalization as well as individuals and families. Our societies necessarily derive from the diverse contributions of all members of our populations, so that unless we interact responsibly and effectively in our families, our societies are weakened. We build better future societies, for example, when we are emotionally secure in our families, as well as more emotionally mature in our family relationships.

Although we cannot change the families we were born into, we can use social intelligence to show us to what extent patterns of behavior in our family and personal histories have influenced our past and present actions. After this important socially intelligent assessment, we can continue to build our social intelligence on firmer foundations of family influences and social facts.

For example, we cannot increase our social intelligence, or become responsible historical actors, unless we first give considerable attention to assessing our family foundations. These are not insignificant details that we can afford to ignore. We need to come to terms with the emotional impacts of our past and present family interactions if we are to gain control over our lives, our goals, and our accomplishments.

Family Processes

Family processes are significant for both social intelligence and societies because families are foundations of our individual and social behavior. Patterns of family interaction are critical influences in how we become human, for example, as well as in how we formulate our highest priorities as individuals and societies. We develop our social awareness and social intelligence in relation to our families' beliefs and values, and we establish our preferred societal goals due to the impacts of family influences on our views of individuals, societies, and the world.

The most important family processes to examine are the repeated patterns of family interaction that influence us the most. These often include interactions that existed in our families before we were born, at the time of our births, and during our formative years as infants, children, adolescents, and young adults. Moreover, social intelligence derives from having sufficient objectivity to recognize and understand the importance of family processes among other powerful, complex social influences such as beliefs, social classes, cultures, and societies.

In all circumstances family processes enable us to be more or less socially intelligent in understanding societies and globalization. Social intelligence uses broad perspectives to clarify how social influences impact our thinking and life outcomes, and social intelligence guides us and societies to establish new goals that increase both the common good and social justice.

Social intelligence is particularly reliable as a means to achieve our goals because it derives from being objective about social influences, and from paying attention to social facts that express the strong impacts of families, beliefs, social classes, cultures, and societies. Because societies are our broadest social contexts for increasing our social intelligence, we necessarily change our understanding of societies at the same time that we apply social intelligence to our thinking. We see our societies more clearly through social intelligence, for example, which includes gaining a deeper understanding of the most recent changes in societies through globalization.

Sometimes it is useful to consider our societies by identifying patterns in broad social processes that are similar to repeated interactions in our families' emotional systems. This helps us to understand the power play among different interest groups within societies as well as among societies. For example, we more easily identify how competing interest groups and societies vie for social advantages, sometimes through social class mobility. Because the emotional bases of our family dependencies are reflected in varied social groups and societies, knowing what family emotional processes are like helps us to recognize emotional reactivity both within and among societies.

Our focus on family processes provides us with views of the foundations of our societies, and of possibilities for changing our societies through interacting differently in our families and other social settings. Thus, as well as being mechanisms which help to bring about broad social changes in societies, family processes may reinforce or transform the family foundations of societies. Furthermore, changing family processes in our families and societies increases our social intelligence. For example, when we become more aware of how much societies need well-functioning families, we are motivated to increase families' flexibility by opening up families' emotional systems.

When we are confused or disgruntled about the lack of progress we make in increasing the common good or achieving social justice, we learn more about what we can do to rectify the complexities of these situations when we return to examining and participating in family processes, or in more widespread emotional processes in societies. For example, the breadth of perspective that social intelligence brings to our decision-making and goals, helps us to be more effective in accomplishing our intentions in spite of restrictive repetitions in family and societal emotional processes. Consequently, we succeed in reaching our goals for social justice in societies by strengthening our immunity to others' reactivity to our different initiatives to increase the common good.

We become more socially intelligent when we are more adept in confronting and dealing with the power and complexities of family emotional processes. For example, we are more likely to achieve social justice goals in societies when we use social intelligence to stay our ground, refuse to be drawn into others' expectations or demands, and focus on our deliberately chosen preferred goals. Thus our efforts to increase our social intelligence gradually enable us to change or even transform our societies in particular respects, so that institutionalized ways of doing things become more flexible and more just for more people.

Family Changes

Because families are such vital social sources and basic foundations of our social intelligence, and because examining family experiences deepens our understanding of ourselves and our goals, we need to be able to change problematic interactions with our families. For example, it is important to know how to go about accomplishing significant family changes, at least in terms of modifying our relationships with family members, so that we increase our social intelligence and strengthen our autonomy. Exercising freedom is a crucial aspect of being socially intelligent, and responsible historical actors need to use freedom and reason in their collective efforts to plan better worlds for the present and future.

Ideally families launch their children into society successfully as they become adults, so that their young family members orient their lives more directly toward accomplishing societal goals which increase the common good and serve social justice. If families do not achieve this, however, their children and young adults predictably remain too dependent on other family members.

Loosening the tight patterns of interdependence in these families helps to free family members who are trapped in too much family togetherness or suffocating closeness. For example, these relatively closed family emotional systems are opened up by making their family bonds more flexible. Social intelligence shows us that when families' emotional systems are less tight and restrictive, all family members may become sufficiently free to assist more directly in significant lifetime tasks such as making societies more egalitarian, inclusive, diverse, cooperative, and open.

The processes necessary for changing ourselves and our families, so that they become more open and flexible, are both complex and daunting. For example, making contact with increased numbers of family members—in order to dilute the intensity of dependencies in families—is often resisted by relatives who are accustomed to repeating problematic dependency patterns of behavior generation after generation. However, if we do nothing to create or maintain open flexible relationships in our families, patterns of behavior we established as children may be replayed in various guises when we are adults. Therefore, we need to be single-minded in our endeavors to form reliable family foundations for our social intelligence, so that we increase our social intelligence and become more effective in our societies.

When we manage to make changes in our families which increase the independence of as many family members as possible, we are more responsible historical actors who develop meaningful missions in societies. However, we do not leave our families behind when we orient our actions toward serving social justice, for example, but rather continue to maintain open family connections so that we can go about our work in societies without being unduly restricted by our families' needs.

The overall purposes of our families are to prepare family members for useful and fulfilling lives in society. Just as social intelligence is a means to accomplish our goals to increase the common good, at best our families are sources of security, inspiration, and companionship rather than ends in themselves. Social intelligence helps us to see our lives from the broad perspectives of families, beliefs, social classes, cultures, and societies, which show families as strategic social sources for understanding connections between families and societies. For example, as family members we necessarily share global experiences and global social realities with other families, as well as make unique contributions to the common good and social justice.

In order to become more socially intelligent we learn about other families as well as our own, particularly families from contrasting social classes, cultures, and time periods. However, we find that in spite of the infinite variety of family forms and processes, for example, there are many significant shared experiences among families, especially with regard to family members' patterns of dependency through time across different generations. Our tasks to learn about families include recognizing the strategic importance of patterns in family dependencies, so that we can act differently to make these patterns more viable for present and future generations of families.

When we make family changes that open up our family dependencies successfully, we benefit other family members and other families by describing our know-how about these improvements. Recognizing significant common denominators of family experiences increases our social intelligence and creates a larger, stronger common good based on social justice. Thus changing our families connects us to societies, and increases possibilities for better worlds tomorrow. When we reduce our families' dependencies, we envision better futures more clearly, and work more effectively with others.

Beliefs and Actions

Our beliefs are a second strand of social intelligence, which works together with the powerful complex social influences of families, social classes, cultures, and societies. Beliefs are significant because they motivate us and direct our actions either toward the common good and social justice, or toward maintaining the status quo of inequities and problem-ridden social issues. Social intelligence helps us to become more aware of our beliefs, for example, so that we live more fully as citizens of our societies, civilizations, and global communities.

Social intelligence recognizes the power and complexities of all religious and secular beliefs, because they both motivate us and direct our goals and behavior. However, because some of our beliefs are stronger than others—or more rigid or more flexible than others—they have varied consequences for our actions.

Social intelligence teaches us that we need to harbor constructive rather than destructive beliefs, because contrasts in their consequences for our actions are both stark and transformative with regard to the qualities of our individual or collective lives. Moreover, we are only truly responsible in our behavior when we select constructive beliefs as motivations and orientations for our actions, because this enables us to asses to what extent we are increasing the common good and social justice.

Changing our beliefs, so that they are as constructive as possible, starts by heightening our awareness of our existing beliefs—such as beliefs about societies as well as beliefs about individuals, groups, and communities. For example, the assumptions we make about human nature and societies are usually buried among our most deep-seated beliefs. Therefore, we must examine these assumptions as fully as possible within the sum total of our beliefs, in order to select our most meaningful beliefs to guide our actions.

However, whether or not we become aware of all our beliefs, our beliefs inevitably continue to drive our actions. Consequently, being socially intelligent includes examining our beliefs, deliberately selecting socially intelligent beliefs, and changing our beliefs. By contrast, acting without deliberately using social intelligence predictably expresses our mismatched or contradictory beliefs.

When we turn to social intelligence to guide our behavior, as well as persist in our efforts to develop social intelligence, we improve our effectiveness in aligning our beliefs and actions. For example, when we are socially intelligent, random beliefs cannot compel us to act in directions we do not want to take. Only when we are not in charge of which beliefs we nurture and express do our less preferred beliefs take over our lives, by dominating our decisions and actions.

When we examine our beliefs closely, including our beliefs about societies, we acknowledge the extent to which both our religious and secular beliefs derive from our families, social classes, cultures, and societies. All the beliefs we harbor have consequences for us and our societies, and we automatically continue to absorb societal beliefs from a wide range of social sources. However, although our families, social classes, cultures, and societies yield both religious and secular beliefs, when we want to understand the social origins of our beliefs—and their impacts on our actions—we start with how we were encouraged to view ourselves and our worlds through our families.

When our families' beliefs consist of social ideals, we may be able to live up to them through our actions. Because parents frequently present particular standards and ideals to us through their expectations for our behavior and accomplishments, their unrealistic demands may still dominate how we behave as adults. Social intelligence helps us to loosen this family hold over our actions. For example, when we exercise our social intelligence by taking more responsibility for formulating our own beliefs, standards, ideals, and actions, we become sufficiently free to pursue far-reaching goals such as increasing the common good and social justice.

Social intelligence shows us that societies need individuals to believe in the well-being of all members of their populations in order to thrive. By contrast, when our beliefs are weighed down by family expectations and family needs, we cannot respond fully to the basic needs of societies. Achieving balance between our families, beliefs, social classes, cultures, and societies is necessary for both individual and societal well-being, especially because new social designs are needed to embrace globalization in modern societies.

Beliefs as Motivations

Just as beliefs are necessarily expressed through our actions, beliefs also fuel our most cherished intentions. For example our beliefs give us reasons to pursue particular goals so that we aim more directly at goals like the common good or social justice. Furthermore, beliefs not only prompt us to act in certain directions, but they also give us meaningful explanations for our actions, reasons to do one thing over another, and purposes to pursue goals when we find it difficult to persist in working toward them.

Social intelligence requires that we analyze and criticize our beliefs because they are our most easily identified sources of our actions. With respect to societies, social intelligence suggests that the dominant beliefs of a particular society make many people's actions fairly predictable in that society. Moreover, being socially intelligent requires that we change our beliefs when needed, in order to accomplish what we prefer and change societies. For example, sometimes special interest groups try to modify other people's beliefs—through formal or informal education—in order to persuade them to accept and promote particular changes in societies.

Historically, transforming people's beliefs is a powerful social and political strategy. In fact, revolutions may start, or political leaders may be ousted, as results of changing people's beliefs and motives. For example, surges of public opinion in societies often express mass beliefs, which are themselves influenced by families, social classes, cultures, and societies. Thus the content and consequences of beliefs may determine the fates of empires or civilizations, because people are motivated to act decisively and effectively according to their strongest beliefs.

Social intelligence considers beliefs as one of the five major social influences in societies because beliefs wield unique powers. Ideally socially intelligent people are fully in charge of their beliefs, so that by deliberately nurturing constructive beliefs, they make effective commitments to work collectively to accomplish their preferred goals. Unfortunately, unless we continue to be alert and aware, and at the same time deliberately cultivate our preferred beliefs as motivations for goal-directed behavior, we may be manipulated and exploited through our beliefs or the beliefs of others. This happens because our beliefs lead us to act in certain ways, and are sources of powerful personal and social influences.

Societies need to motivate entire populations to accept the status quo in sufficient respects to ensure their survival. Shared beliefs encourage us to accept essential social values and procedures which allow our societies to exist and function. However, if there are insufficient shared substantive beliefs, societies are not able to hold their own against the harsh odds of everyday conflicts and rapid social changes.

This is why social intelligence emphasizes the importance of scrutinizing societies' beliefs, in order to make reliable factual assessments of the directions societies are moving in through time. For example, our increased historical awareness of societies' beliefs shows us which beliefs are instrumental in supporting traditional societies, and which beliefs strengthen modern societies. This social intelligence helps us to establish more meaningful links among our individual and social beliefs, motivations, and goals.

If we want to change our societies, we must make careful assessments of beliefs in the status quo as well as beliefs in alternative societies. However, if we move too quickly toward making changes in our societies, by assuming mistakenly that populations are ready for major social changes, our efforts predictably backfire rather than come to fruition.

Beliefs provide us with reliable clues with which to assess the status quo of societies, as well as directions to pursue for bringing about qualitative changes in the ways we organize ourselves. When we know how we and other people in our societies are motivated, we more easily appeal to others' political wills, and design alternative ways to conduct our day-to-day business effectively and responsibly.

We experience our beliefs and motives as being very personal and intimate because they are integral aspects of our most cherished values. Our beliefs and motives also distinguish individuals or groups from each other as either maintaining societies' status quo or creating alternative societies. Thus both our beliefs and our motives link us to societies because they guide us to act in particular ways in relation to societies. For example, if we are socially intelligent, we deliberately select our preferred beliefs to guide us in changing our societies. Consequently we are motivated to achieve individually or collectively chosen constructive goals, because we aim to create better future societies from our present situations.

Beliefs and Goals

Societies depend on their citizens to share beliefs and goals that reinforce their societies' ways of doing things in order to thrive. Our beliefs and goals are therefore critical aspects of societies' existence and fulfillment, whether we realize this or not, because these vital links between individuals, their decisions, their behavior, and their societies create essential social foundations for all. When we share sufficient beliefs with each other, we inevitably share similar goals, with the result that socially intelligent objectives like increasing the common good and achieving social justice are possible.

One way in which societies benefit from nurturing their citizens' beliefs is that societies can more deliberately coordinate their citizens' goals with national and international objectives. Furthermore, when citizens' beliefs are built on an empathic awareness of societies' needs, there may be considerable overlap between individual, group, societal, and international goals. In these respects shared beliefs and goals are essential aspects of the credibility and viability of present and future societies.

When citizens' beliefs reflect social ideals like social justice, societies benefit from the altruism of these goals.

VII. Families and Beliefs

Although it is difficult to imagine how some of our complex modern societies could use ideals like social justice to guide their everyday behavior, it is a viable or optimal possibility.

Social facts underlying our beliefs suggest that to the extent that we deliberately choose our beliefs, we also select our actions, motivations, and goals. Furthermore, when we have sufficient awareness—through techniques like increasing our social intelligence—we are more in charge of our lives, as well as more adept at meeting our needs and the needs of our societies.

Even when societies are distinctly global in their orientations and outreach to other societies, our beliefs do not assume any less significance or importance in relation to creating world well-being. As within our societies, our beliefs must necessarily be outward looking in orientation, so that we can be open to meeting some real needs of other societies as well as our own. Our beliefs must help us to develop social conditions for peaceful co-existence in the world at large, if we are to survive and be fulfilled.

Consequently, we try to nurture beliefs that increase rather than decrease the odds for accomplishing goals that uphold and strengthen the world community. Even though our beliefs may lead us to agree with others about working toward these broad goals, at the same time we need to scrutinize social facts about different societies in order to assess whether our shared beliefs really assist us to achieve our goals. In these respects, cultivating objectivity makes our cooperation with other countries more enlightened, effective, and productive.

When we have socially intelligent intentions to increase the common good and social justice throughout the world, we must set ourselves manageable tasks, so that we can coordinate our beliefs and goals successfully each day. For example, we ask important questions such as how can we communicate with populations, so that socially intelligent reforms will be sufficiently accepted and implemented? Must we wait for world-wide political disasters before we can muster the political will necessary to change our current ways of doing things? Do we have the social intelligence resources necessary to improve meaningful survival and fulfillment throughout the world?

One reliable method to increase the number of people who are willing to move in these constructive directions is to make formal and informal education more available to all members of our populations. Insofar as social intelligence results from educating ourselves and each other about social realities, we realize that we need to give increased attention to priorities that enhance universal education. For example, developing new bodies of knowledge allows us both to value the histories of our societies, and to raise direct questions about how to create better worlds.

It is only by combining the many talents in and among our societies that societies will survive and thrive amidst the ongoing intense social issues that plague today's modern world. The valuable broad social perspectives of societies allow us to more easily see that socially intelligent beliefs lead societies to establish socially intelligent goals, so that societies construct rather than destroy our future worlds. In significant respects, our starting points to set this constructive chain of events in motion are our individual and collective socially intelligent beliefs and goals.

VIII. Social Classes and Cultures

Social classes and cultures are the third and fourth components of social intelligence because they too represent strong social influences throughout societies. Historically we organize societies according to divisions of labor, hierarchies of power, and varied resources, which define specific qualities of life for all members of populations through time. Similarly, values and ideals necessary for everyday survival evolve according to basic social needs, so that rich varieties of cultures develop, sometimes with remarkable degrees of coherence and consistency, as well as conflicts and contradictions.

This chapter of *Societies and Social Intelligence* examines the influences of social classes and cultures in social intelligence and societies. Both social classes and cultures derive in part from the earlier major social and emotional influences of families and beliefs—two other components of social intelligence. Social classes and cultures are also produced by societies, societal beliefs, and societal values. Thus social intelligence is distilled working knowledge based on social facts about all five major social dimensions of families, beliefs, social classes, cultures, and societies.

Social intelligence is a learned capacity which helps us to understand, assess, and deliberately choose how to relate—as individuals, groups, communities, and societies—to the five major social influences of families, beliefs, social classes, cultures, and societies. By scrutinizing social facts resulting from these influences, and by choosing particular social beliefs we want to work with, we become more effective at navigating our lives, and at achieving our preferred goals. Social intelligence enhances our understanding of our societies, so that we are more enlightened historical actors and more resourceful participants in societies.

In order to understand the depth of the impacts that social classes have on defining our opportunities and life chances, we consider how traditional social classes developed, how modern social classes came into being, and how social intelligence guides us to change social classes. In addition, we examine why resistance to changing social classes continues to confront us in societies in most circumstances, and how working together with others toward increasing social justice empowers our efforts to change social classes, especially when we need to reduce opposition.

The impacts of cultures on social classes and societies are also examined in this chapter of *Societies and Social Intelligence*. For example, we first recognize the pervasiveness of our cultures, and then define the consequences that our value choices have for our daily decisions and preferred goals. However, even though cultural influences seem to be fairly independent in their own right, our social intelligence ultimately derives from the interplay of all five major social influences in our lives—families, beliefs, social classes, cultures, and societies.

We are who we are due to the impacts of families, beliefs, social classes, cultures, and societies on how we think and how we act. Because we cannot escape the effects of these influences, our individual and social responsibilities lie primarily in coping with them as effectively as possible, and in using their power and complexities to direct our lives, societies, and future worlds.

In considering why our societies make substantial differences to our approaches to life, and why social intelligence guides us to be more objective and wiser in our value choices, we recognize that social classes and cultures—like families and beliefs—define the well-being of whole populations rather than individuals. For example, it is largely in our roles as citizens that we are considered to have more or less status in relation to others in our societies. Consequently, being a member of an upper social class or a mainstream culture usually gives us more social privileges than other members of societies.

In these respects social classes and cultures uphold inequities in societies, rather than the social justice values of equality, inclusiveness, diversity, cooperation, and openness. When we are socially intelligent, however, we define and carve out more freedom for ourselves, make different social or value choices, and work cooperatively with others to increase social justice. Although not everyone who is socially intelligent proceeds toward similar goals in these endeavors, historical actors aim to create better societies collectively. Furthermore, when we turn to social intelligence for guidance, our actions are based on firm foundations of social facts, as well as on deeper understandings of how societies survive and thrive.

Traditional Social Classes

Social intelligence suggests that we need historical perspectives in order to be objective in our decisions and actions about the present and future. Therefore, when we set ourselves the task of trying to understand social classes more fully—social classes are the third dimension of social intelligence—we need to review our knowledge of social classes in the past, as examples of how to organize societies that we do not necessarily have to repeat in the present or future. Because social intelligence encourages us to assume responsibilities for creating better worlds, so that members of entire populations survive and thrive rather than only members of privileged social classes, we need to seriously consider alternatives to traditional social classes.

In the past and present, social classes are usually more rigid and more central in the organization of traditional societies. For example, members of traditional social classes are clearly distinguished from each other, especially in societies where social classes are based on varying amounts of material assets. There is also more widespread acceptance of the merits of social classes throughout traditional societies. In these contexts, one of the rationales for the existence of clear-cut social classes is that they are thought of as solid foundations for the security of traditional societies, as well as essential for societies' survival and prosperity.

Some of the more invisible aspects of traditional social classes are social class memberships based on having or not having social connections with high status individuals who have rich financial resources and special privileges. For example, where patronage is widespread, families or individual family members may be assisted sufficiently to make satisfactory livings. In modern societies, the good graces of benefactors and philanthropists continue to neutralize some traditional social class inequalities.

Traditional social classes are often based on gender and age as well as material resources and social connections. It is only in relatively recent modern societies that mass social movements focus on social issues related to genders and sexual orientations, or on political policies to increase social benefits for elderly citizens. However, from the points of view of evolution and history, social classes based on genders and ages have been powerful in distinguishing social differences consistently through time.

In spite of longstanding social class differences based on gender and age, social facts about early and contemporary hunting and gathering societies show that women and men often led qualitatively distinct but fairly egalitarian lives. When these geographically mobile societies settle, however, they gradually transform their egalitarian communities into male dominated hierarchical social classes and societies.

Religions are additional bases of traditional social classes, even though some religions largely unify small societies rather than encourage competitive social classes. For example, religious beliefs provide rationales for the existence of varied social classes, because societies frequently depend on social classes to establish social order in societies. Religions reinforce social classes because they view hierarchical orders of social classes as necessary and natural for societies, thereby being God-given and holy.

In most circumstances traditional social classes are generally upheld—without much resistance—by traditional societies. This support of the status quo in societies with traditional social classes extends the acceptance of traditional social class differences, and dampens efforts to bring about socially intelligent changes in social classes and societies.

However, this religious and social reinforcement of traditional social classes need not compel us to maintain the status quo of traditional social classes now, but rather guides us to take responsible action to reorganize social classes. It is in a spirit of inquiry into better futures that social intelligence helps us to critically assess diverse patterns in traditional social classes of the past and present more accurately. Furthermore, social intelligence invites us to design alternative ways to organize ourselves in the present for the future, in order to avoid repeating our mistakes of the past with regard to traditional social classes.

One of the moral principles that social intelligence uses to reform current social class inequities is social justice. When we apply social justice to our concerns about the inherent inequities of traditional social classes, we see new ways to at least close some of the ever-widening gaps between those who have abundant material resources, and those who have insufficient material means. Social justice also guides us to consider additional viable alternatives to traditional social classes, so that more egalitarian futures are assured, as well as better social conditions for all in future societies.

Modern Social Classes

Even though modern social classes are usually more open than traditional social classes, they often resist social changes, have limited social mobility, and are difficult to change. One characteristic of social classes in modern societies is that there are more different social classes in modern societies, with varied social class bases, than in traditional societies. This means that modern social classes support and express the diversity of modern societies to some extent, but at the same time they restrict social opportunities in order to maintain complex hierarchical social class arrangements.

Examples of the multiple social class bases of modern social classes include social classes based on education, occupation, race, ethnicity, ablebodiedness, and sexual orientation as well as the more traditional social class bases of material resources, social connections, religions, genders, and ages. Social intelligence shows us that recent social classes in modern societies have overlapping allegiances, which often make rankings among modern social classes more difficult to identify and understand than traditional social classes.

Even though irregular patterns of exchanges emerge in these overlapping modern social classes, each of the multiplied bases of social classes has its own hierarchical order. Furthermore, all modern social classes have marked contrasts between upper and lower rankings within their different social classes.

Social intelligence helps us to appreciate the substantive differences between traditional and modern social classes, as well as recognizes the similar ways in which some modern social classes are as competitive as traditional social classes. We also need to acknowledge that traditional social classes are perpetuated by modern societies.

Social intelligence shows us that shifts in social classes through time have occurred due to societies' needs to adapt to significant trends both within their populations and among societies, especially during globalization. Therefore, at best the increase in modern social class bases helps modern societies to adapt to widespread current social conditions.

In spite of these constructive functions and accomplishments of modern social classes, the hierarchical arrangements within modern social classes present as many social issues and social problems as traditional social classes. For example, the unequal social hierarchy within each modern social class system ultimately fosters widespread discontent with these broad social arrangements in modern societies. Furthermore, the social conditions of modern social classes often result in alienation, so that cooperative communities—which are relatively equal, inclusive, diverse, and open—cannot easily take root.

Social intelligence suggests that both traditional and modern social classes need to be changed in order to increase the common good and social justice. Unless we deliberately put focused thought and effort into designing different ways to organize our societies, both traditional and modern social classes will reproduce themselves and support the status quo of unfair and undesirable inequalities.

From the point of view of the overall welfare of our societies—even though both traditional and modern social classes may maintain social solidarity and equilibrium in societies in the short run—dissatisfactions with both traditional and modern social classes will predictably outweigh their advantages. For example, when the destructive consequences of modern social classes emerge, societies are sometimes impaired in their development and cannot adapt successfully in globalization.

Social intelligence suggests that only by deliberately modifying our modern social classes, as well as the traditional social classes that persist in modern societies, are we able to construct social conditions that create better futures. Strategies to accomplish this include increasing the common good and social justice by designing new ways to neutralize or narrow gaps between the privileges and disadvantages among different social classes. Therefore, we cannot afford to be complacent about the variety of bases in modern social classes, because they unavoidably lead to intense competitiveness and diminished life satisfaction.

In some respects societies can improve the social consequences of both traditional and modern social classes through changing priorities in their political and social policies. For example, when we devote national resources to creating more egalitarian opportunities, we ultimately benefit all people in these societies. This move is effective in the long run, however, only when we design comprehensive services that resolve social deprivations. These support services allow us to undo some of the destructive consequences of both traditional and modern social classes.

However, before such critical adjustments are possible, we need to educate ourselves about existing social classes and socially intelligent options for changing social classes. Increasing our social intelligence improves our effectiveness, and helps us to work more cooperatively with others to achieve the important goals of designing alternatives for both traditional and modern social classes.

Changing Social Classes

When we understand links between social intelligence and societies more fully, we can go about making constructive changes in societies through changing social classes. Furthermore, to the extent that we undertake socially intelligent strategies to regulate the most destructive consequences of social classes, for example, the achievement of our goals will create better societies for the future.

A first step in undertaking these objectives is to collect facts about the most extreme social class contrasts in contemporary societies, and their consequences for societies' populations. We then need to assess our social resources and our access to additional social resources, in order to minimize or neutralize unfair social class contrasts. Although it does not make sense to dream too much about ideals for existing social classes in the early stages of our socially intelligent efforts, in due course we may design effective acceptable alternatives to current social classes.

These plans are built on the socially intelligent premise that because we learn our social classes, they can be changed through trial and error approaches to constructing options to our established social classes. For example, if we continue to educate ourselves formally and informally about societies and social classes, we gradually learn how to undo at least some of the most destructive consequences of our current social class arrangements.

Social intelligence helps us to see links between families, beliefs, social classes, cultures, and societies. Social intelligence also suggests that if we are to change our societies through changing our social classes, we must become more objective about our social resources and options. We need to be aware that aiming to increase the common good and social justice can motivate us to pursue the very difficult and challenging tasks involved in making these changes in social classes and societies.

Social intelligence helps us to be more effective historical actors. For example, we increase our understanding of past, present, and future social classes as we work toward changing social classes through coordinated actions. We use past facts to orient us to the present, as well as present facts to orient us to the future. This enables us to construct more just social arrangements for future societies.

Being historical actors makes us more responsible in what we choose to do, because we now make more accurate assessments about the consequences of our actions before we act. We also become more able to find like-minded others, so that we proceed effectively toward our goals through socially intelligent cooperation. We are all historical actors, whether we realize this or not. However, when we heighten our awareness about being historical actors, we predictably increase our effectiveness, as well as the likelihood that we will be successful in changing social classes.

If we think that changing social classes is impossible, we need to consider how emotional processes affect this goal. For example, to what extent is our lack of progress due to others' resistance, or to their emotional pressures to conform to traditional expectations about social classes? How can we break through the hold of the powerful social influences of social classes, so that we continue to strive for preferred ideals and goals? How does viewing society as a whole improve the likelihood of achieving these possibilities for changing social classes? Can we find others who share our goals, so that we work cooperatively and effectively with them to achieve social class changes?

Social intelligence helps us to persist in our aims to improve our societies through changing social classes. For example, we deal with social realities that face us more objectively and more appropriately when we use social facts to deepen our understanding of social classes and societies. Furthermore, the broad contexts of social intelligence help us to both visualize and work toward improving our shared futures.

In order to stay motivated and oriented to achieving our goals of changing social classes, we keep our new priorities firmly in place by making new value choices on a daily basis. Also, social intelligence shows us how to deepen our appreciation of the power of our cultures in societies, by understanding how our value choices influence who we are, what we do, and how we accomplish our goals. When we increase our social intelligence, for example, we gain additional control over our value choices, which ultimately influences how we change our social classes and societies.

Traditional Cultures

Culture is the fourth strand of social intelligence, which is based on the premise that social intelligence derives from our working knowledge of the five major social influences of families, beliefs, social classes, cultures, and societies. In this context, culture is considered as a particular broad vista of society, because culture underpins all the social structures and processes in societies with values, knowledge, and ideals that bestow meanings on our everyday exchanges with others.

Both traditional and modern cultures hold our current societies in place, because societies' values are significant social sources of our orientations, motives, and social actions. Due to the fact that both traditional and modern cultures have distinctive qualities, it is useful to identify some of these differences. Also, because we want to see how social intelligence changes our understanding of societies, and how we can change our societies through our cultures, we need to know how both traditional and modern cultures relate to changing cultures.

Traditional cultures include the first known cultural artifacts and cultural practices from our earliest communities to the present, as well as more sophisticated values associated with our earliest civilizations. Traditional cultures and cultural practices were and still are largely focused on our immediate survival as families, communities, and societies, or on local life cycle rituals which help people to deal with births, deaths, and transitions such as youth to adulthood or middle age to old age. Gender contrasts in traditional cultures mark different social expectations for boys and girls or men and women, which usually continue for a lifetime.

In addition to the social needs and community orientations that traditional cultures meet, traditional cultures and traditional cultural values instill repeated patterns of interaction that are frequently passed down from generation to generation. Thus cultural values are sustained beyond single lifetimes. Traditional cultures are frequently so distinct and visible in everyday life that they are experienced as the only true social order of societies. For example, when religious beliefs overlap traditional cultural beliefs, a tribe's or a community's world view is reinforced by sacred rituals and sanctions as well as by social customs.

For our purposes here it is enough to appreciate the depth of the traditional cultural roots that underlie our experiences of our societies. For example, if we are irked by the slow pace of change in some areas of our lives in contemporary societies, we need to consider the historical origins of our everyday cultural meanings, so that we are more objective about cultural and social realities that have persisted from distant pasts to the present. Social intelligence also reminds us that the traditional cultural cores of our contemporary societies frequently resist change and persist with their own momentums, in spite of our planned individual and collective efforts to bring about changes.

Traditional values usually derive from relatively homogeneous cultures that promote survival for communities in local social conditions. Consequently, unlike the cultures and values of modern mass societies, the values of traditional cultures are tightly-knit, and relate particularly to small local communities rather than modern global societies.

In order to understand to what extent the dynamics of cultural changes affect today's societies, we must first identify the parts played by traditional cultures in relation to modern cultures in our societies. In fact, it is often because of the predictable clashes between the values of traditional and modern cultures that many cultural and social changes occur in contemporary societies today. In these respects our cultures not only suggest new directions for our societies to take, but they also help us to assess the success or failure of our adaptations to globalization, and the political tensions that traditional and modern cultures produce.

Traditional cultures, because of their central importance to societies' well-being, provide us with starting points for assessing the wide range of historical changes that societies have experienced, as well as their accompanying cultural changes. The most significant traditional cultures express ranges of value choices that confront populations and societies throughout history. For example, we critically examine closed traditional cultures with their emphases on hierarchies of social honor, exclusiveness, and homogeneity, so that we are better prepared to usher in open modern cultures that support equality, inclusiveness, diversity, and cooperation.

Modern Cultures

Varied modern cultures are found everywhere in today's societies. Moreover, if societies have survived to the present, they are necessarily integral parts of the ongoing international global community which reflects the modern world and modern cultures. Because technological discoveries have made world travel relatively easy and not necessarily prohibitively expensive, more and more individuals and populations traverse the world and live as cosmopolitan world citizens.

This is the distinctive landscape of modern cultures. When we examine these rapid social changes and changing societies, we grasp the enormity of the cultural changes that have occurred during the last two centuries. Furthermore, because we are historical actors, social intelligence encourages us to stand up and make responsible decisions about our value choices amidst the pervasive modern cultures in which we live.

In order to simplify our complex social situations sufficiently to understand some of the basic dynamics of cultural and social changes, modern cultures are often thought of as the opposite of traditional cultures. However, the pace of societies' changes throughout the world increased considerably in past decades, so we cannot predict modern cultures accurately for the next fifty or one hundred years. The social conditions required for the development of modern cultures change dramatically in relatively short periods of time, and it is difficult to even envision what future cultures will be like unless we make some planned interventions.

In light of these rapidly changing circumstances, social intelligence requires that we make a few useful broad assessments of cultural changes, without allowing ourselves to be drawn into the quagmires of existing cultural variations. For example, because cultural change possibilities seem to be infinite, it does not behoove us to spell out exactly what particular variations might be. Rather, we should intervene in cultural processes, so that we are surer that our preferred values become widely recognized value choices within these complex change processes.

Social intelligence suggests that above all it is important to develop a clear working knowledge of patterns in cultural changes in our societies through time, so that we both discern and opt for values that have the most productive cultural and social outcomes. For example, if we use our social intelligence to contribute to the common good and social justice more directly, we focus on constructive social ideals—such as equality, inclusiveness, diversity, cooperation, and openness—because they are integral to successful modern cultures.

VIII. Social Classes and Cultures

Social intelligence shows us that even though modern cultures have infinitely more social values than traditional cultures, it is not particularly fruitful to define, describe, and explain what modern cultural values are. Rather, we need to be sufficiently socially intelligent to focus on specific cultural values that will save us from drowning in the infinite variety of cultural values in modern societies.

Also important for our modern cultures and value choices is the need to see the present as a culmination of the past, as well as a preparation for the future. Social intelligence prompts us to understand modern cultures as well as traditional cultures, so that we are sufficiently discriminating to nurture values that foster societies' survival and fulfillment. For example, equality, inclusiveness, diversity, cooperation, and openness derive from both traditional and modern cultures, and create optimal social conditions for building modern societies according to social justice principles.

Social intelligence establishes a productive momentum for creating viable societies that embrace globalization, and for nurturing constructive values to survive and be fulfilled. Because we need peaceful coexistence among societies to survive and be fulfilled, we must discover and make cultural choices that promote these social conditions. Our future worlds do not evolve from a vacuum. Social intelligence enhances our awareness and wisdom, and directs our collective actions toward changing our cultures and societies constructively for the future.

Although religious values can point out ways to achieve these endeavors—as well as social intelligence, the common good, and social justice—the secular, more objective cultural values of social intelligence often promote equality, inclusiveness, diversity, cooperation, and openness throughout populations more successfully. These particular value choices are cultural ideals that reflect social justice, and therefore orient us effectively toward making meaningful and successful cultural changes for constructive futures. This is especially important because indirect cultural changes can change both traditional and modern societies in the long run.

Changing Cultures

An important consideration in thinking about our societies and their changing cultures is the kinds of changes that human beings initiate—or deal with—amidst complex cultural and social processes. Although social intelligence focuses primarily on cultural changes that affect societies as well as cultures, we can also surmise that many cultural changes occur as adaptations to historical changes both within and outside our societies. However, cultures remain as important and powerful agents of social change and social intelligence.

For example, technological discoveries encourage inventions that change the information members of societies have access to each day, so that new patterns in communications generate qualitative changes in our cultures and societies. As we cope with modern technologies through our twenty-first century lifestyles, we find that some technologies are not only powerful and pervasive but increasingly required in societies, in order to function in the business world or even in our personal lives. These cultural changes happen in spite of ourselves, and may pull us along reluctantly because of their powerful momentums.

Social intelligence recommends that we accept these aspects of our information revolution as positively as possible, so that we are not weakened through our resistance to modern cultures and values. Our socially intelligent emphasis needs to be on the extent to which we apply these new technologies to how we organize our daily routines, and how we work alone or with others. In some respects we must keep up with mainstream societies merely so that we are not left behind in the midst of rapid cultural changes.

VIII. Social Classes and Cultures

In these conditions of accepting changing cultures rather than trying to change cultures ourselves, we continue to use social intelligence to guide our value choices, so that we directly or indirectly reinforce constructive values like equality, inclusiveness, diversity, cooperation, and openness. When we deepen our commitments to express these value choices, we find increased opportunities to do so on a daily basis. Clearing our heads of the complexities of ongoing cultural choices enables us to focus on directions we really want to take in creating improved cultures and better societies for the future.

When we have specific goals to accomplish for social justice, or aim to increase the common good, we need to remain steadfast to particular value choices that we believe will construct better worlds. For example, we use equality, inclusiveness, diversity, cooperation, and openness to show us how to make decisions and act, at the same time that we design and implement specific changes in our cultures. Thus social intelligence guides us to make fuller use of our cultural means to bring about cultural and social changes. Furthermore, because we learn our cultures, we can unlearn their problematic aspects.

Social intelligence suggests that our preferred goals gradually become new social realities when we establish changing cultures as priorities. Furthermore, we need to know our cultural starting points as well as our cultural goals when we implement cultural changes, so that we retain some control over the directions of our efforts.

The broad perspectives of social intelligence also show us that cultural changes often become societal changes, because our traditional and modern cultures reveal new options for constructive social changes. Consequently, when we focus on the substantive values of our traditional and modern cultures, we develop more successful ways to intervene in our societies, so that we increase the common good and social justice for all.

As historical actors who understand the depth of our cultural roots, we are routinely more effective at bringing about social changes when we focus on the meaningful significance of our cultures. Cultures are avenues which both increase our awareness of social issues, and bring about effective cultural and social changes. Therefore, when we address the cultural hearts of others, we make progress in reforming social problems in our societies.

Our cultures help us to understand complex social realities. However few or many social problems societies have, cultural issues underpin the facts and figures of specific problematic situations. Moreover, our cultures open up our communications about social issues, and allow us to see our societies differently. Consequently, social intelligence encourages us to use our cultures to make substantive changes in our social conditions for ourselves and for members of future generations.

IX. Social Justice

Although social justice is not one of the five major social influences—families, beliefs, social classes, cultures, and societies—that create and sustain our social intelligence, social justice is a significant direction that is inspired by social intelligence. Whereas social intelligence is necessarily a tool which helps us to live more fully, by accomplishing goals that we decide will increase the common good of societies, social justice is a moral ideal that motivates us to live more fully in order to create better worlds in the future.

We all have some degree of social intelligence in order to survive as members of our societies. Moreover, we can all change our relationships to our societies by deliberately cultivating our social intelligence. For example, we increase our awareness of societies and how they work when we strengthen our social intelligence through scrutinizing the major social influences of families, beliefs, social classes, cultures, and societies. Seeing and living through these broad perspectives enables us to appreciate what social justice is, and how necessary social justice is for increasing the common good in our present and future societies.

Thus social intelligence moves us toward social justice, and social justice helps us to achieve goals we choose through increasing our social intelligence. Furthermore, we tend to find likeminded others when we start to move in directions that increase social justice, because our shared value choices inspire collective ventures to establish equality, inclusiveness, diversity, cooperation, and openness in our societies. These qualities of social life increase opportunities for others, and at the same time decrease alienation from fractured families, dogmatic beliefs, restrictive social classes, destructive cultural values, and dysfunctional societies.

As we become more socially intelligent, we prepare ourselves to assume commitments and responsibilities that nurture social justice. To the extent that we strengthen our social intelligence, we clarify our visions of societies, and make decisions to work collectively with others as responsible historical actors.

Even though we are all historical actors, only when we are awake to the many challenges of being historical actors can we achieve social justice effectively. Social intelligence continues to sharpen our social awareness, and motivates us to persevere in working toward social justice, amidst the powerful and complex major social influences of families, beliefs, social classes, cultures, and societies.

Our deeper socially intelligent understanding helps us to realize that it is easier to increase the common good of societies when we move in directions of social justice. For example, we see that achieving selfish competitive goals does not facilitate our collective survival in the long run, and that personal satisfaction can only derive from doing whatever we can to secure the well-being of all. The social facts we learn as we become more socially intelligent orient us toward social justice, so that we more easily find creative and effective ways to meet goals that enhance the quality of life in our societies and civilizations.

We embrace social justice ideals in order to proceed more effectively toward achieving shared collective goals to increase the common good. We may also decide to change major social influences in our societies, so that our societies are stronger and less destructive in globalization. For example, we directly or indirectly describe social intelligence to those who are trapped in their families, beliefs, social classes, cultures, and societies, so that they become aware historical actors who start to work toward creating better societies.

Social justice is an important goal of increased social intelligence because it transcends the pressures and conflicts in our immediate social situations. We cannot pursue only social intelligence, because this is merely a means to an end. For example, we become more socially intelligent in order to serve others more meaningfully and more fairly. Sometimes turning toward social justice reveals purposes that enhance others' lives that we had not realized before, so then we proceed more ably to achieve goals which ensure better futures for our societies.

Before examining how we can change our societies in these ways, as discussed in the final section of *Societies and Social Intelligence,* **Changing Societies**, we look more closely at social justice and its connections to social intelligence. Each of the subsections in this present chapter of *Societies and Social Intelligence* highlights the significance of the common good, families, beliefs, social classes, cultures, and being historical actors in relation to social justice.

Social Justice and the Common Good

Social justice is a moral ideal which transcends the everyday needs of particular societies. It is a beacon that guides multiple efforts to establish fairer societies within and among societies in the world community. Although social justice can be fought for and won or achieved in individual societies, the implications and consequences of social justice reach far beyond national boundaries in globalization.

By contrast, the common good is frequently considered to be accomplished through political means in particular societies. Whereas social justice, a moral ideal, has no tangible boundaries or limits for its impacts and concerns, the common good is often more tangible and specific— for example, the common good usually relates directly to particular nation states or societies during specific time periods. Moreover, whereas social justice sometimes has clear global dimensions, the common good is more consistently basic to the daily functioning of societies, and historically reflects distributions of means and well-being within societies.

Although social justice continues to guide societies whether or not it is accomplished by them, the common good meets societies' expectations that current goals must be met now, in order to conduct the ongoing business of societies' everyday life. Thus the common good is not only the nuts and bolts of political policies, but it is also the orientation we need to deal effectively with necessities related to our survival, practical goals, and social expectations.

In some real respects, the common good makes the existing world go round, whereas social justice inspires us to create better worlds. Social intelligence helps us to deal with current social conditions, social situations, and social issues, so that we produce a sufficiently adequate common good for all in our societies. Furthermore, because both the common good and social justice may ultimately express universal concerns, we cannot increase our social intelligence without at least aiming to meet the needs of other members of our families, other societies, and the world.

Consequently, to a certain extent social justice overlaps with the common good, so that social intelligence helps us to appreciate differences in the scope of outreach of both the common good and social justice. Whereas social justice addresses infinite existential conditions, and its values guide us to produce better worlds, the common good is more limited in scope, and focuses largely on how we meet our most practical survival needs now.

When we are socially intelligent, our value choices are often determined by concerns for both the common good and social justice. For example, our commitments to the common good and social justice help us to assume individual and collective responsibilities to achieve their particular goals. Because the goals of the common good and social justice are compatible with one another, they necessarily lead us to create better societies.

Societies benefit a great deal from citizens who are socially intelligent, and who commit themselves to pursue the common good and social justice as historical actors. Although societies predictably resist many innovations and designs for substantial social changes in how people interact and accomplish their daily tasks, in the long run societies depend on the breadth of vision of historical actors, in order to stay strong and healthy in the world community and globalization. For example, societies need both dreamers and doers, in order to reform or resolve existing social problems. This prevents societies from imploding or exploding into social destruction or extinction.

To the extent that focusing on societies' common good may be myopic or ethnocentric, social justice reminds us that our goals must ultimately be universal, so that we can make far-reaching changes to achieve better worlds. Therefore, just as cultivating social intelligence gives us broader perspectives from which to view ourselves and our societies, social justice gives us broader perspectives from which to understand the common good and our responsibilities to achieve universal goals. We are who we are not only because of what we do on a daily basis, but also because of what we aim for each day.

In many respects increasing our social intelligence is for naught if we do not also consider the common good and social justice. Because humans are social beings, we need meaningful goals to transcend our everyday chores as we keep our lives in motion. For example, we benefit from serving others as well as by giving our socially intelligent know-how to others, because we know that what we do makes our societies fairer and more equitable for the next generation. This is the promise of socially intelligent value choices—such as equality, inclusiveness, diversity, cooperation, and openness—for our future societies and the world.

Social Justice and Families

Social justice guides our families as well as our societies, especially in the sphere of showing families how to launch their family members into accomplishing varied societal tasks. We no longer rear our children to stay at home with our families in modern societies, because our horizons have broadened through time. In fact, in order to live fully, we encourage our children—and other family members—to engage in activities that connect them with broad social purposes such as social justice.

Although the intensity of our families' emotional systems often makes it difficult for family members to tackle family issues or conflicts about what is just and fair within our own families, this is a significant task of being socially intelligent. We need to understand our families sufficiently, for example, so that we can open up our families to be sufficiently equal, inclusive, diverse, cooperative, and open to function well and support the well-being of all family members. Because our families are our first arenas to understand, know, and apply our social intelligence, we change our behavior in our families in ways that aim to free both us and other family members.

Because families all too often trap their members in unproductive relationships or damaging patterns of behavior, we first need to be alert to what our habitual ways of relating to our families are. Having a perspective of social justice helps us to be more objective about how our identities and everyday tasks were originally defined by our families. For example, we try to answer questions such as do our families have divisions of labor that protect only some of our family members' well-being, while at the same time they exploit or oppress others? Can we define ourselves more clearly so that we communicate what it is that we are willing and unwilling to do in relation to meeting the needs of our more dependent family members?

Social justice helps us to focus on our socially intelligent efforts and goals more directly, so that we become more effective both within and outside our families. The balance we need to achieve, in our responsibilities as historical actors who are pursuing social justice, is that we have obligations to both our family members and members of societies. Thus social justice helps us to be more decisive and fairer in allocating our socially intelligent time and energies to particular family or social tasks.

Social justice also enables us to discern more clearly what our social responsibilities are as women and men, and as young or old people. For example, do we accept the traditional roles of women and men in our families, or do we concentrate more on becoming strong individuals who select their orienting values very carefully? Do we make accommodations to particular ages as we progress through the life cycle, or do we establish socially intelligent life-long goals and commitments? In the long run social intelligence guides us to act according to our own motives to change ourselves and the world. Consequently, we take as much freedom as we can get to be our best selves as historical actors, whatever our genders or ages.

We also need to make decisions about social justice in how we act as adult children of elderly parents, or as spouses, brothers, sisters, nieces, nephews, and cousins in our families. Social intelligence suggests that we benefit from playing these roles independently, without striving to meet conventional expectations. For example, when we let social justice guide us, role-playing is much less significant than our primary goal of working toward social justice.

Even though social intelligence gives us dependable practical knowledge as well as reliable strategies to increase the common good, we cannot force others to do our will when applying social intelligence to our own lives. For example, we may think that we have answers to taxing social issues, because we have deliberately increased our own social intelligence, but we do not have the right to tell others what to do unless they need protection or ask us for guidance. However, because we necessarily communicate our concerns and enlightenment through our deeds, acting in directions to increase social justice becomes an example which often inspires others who are interested in developing purposes or directions in their everyday lives.

Social Justice and Beliefs

Societies are directly affected by their populations' beliefs. For example, populations in modern industrial societies often focus on personal day-to-day comforts because businesses use social facts about consumer behavior to impact our cultures and expand profits, rather than increase national well-being. Political elites may also control societies through fostering beliefs that support particular societal priorities and policies which may or may not be in societies' long term interests. Consequently, believing that enjoying our personal lives is our highest good, or that our most powerful politicians know best, lays groundwork for ignoring our own responsibilities for the common good and social justice.

By contrast, living according to beliefs which encourage us to participate fully in our democratic rights and responsibilities to construct our preferred societies, provides societies with completely different foundational beliefs. These change-oriented beliefs motivate populations to choose and create opportunities for all. In these circumstances we define our well-being through expressing altruism or pragmatic values to ensure the fulfillment of all members of our societies. Furthermore, societies with these constructive beliefs move with new and vigorous momentums, which enable their populations to be more responsible in pursuing the common good and social justice.

Social intelligence helps us to discern and understand different outcomes of our beliefs, and at the same time points us toward increasing the common good and social justice. For example, when sufficient facts are collected about social class differences in societies, we see that morally and pragmatically societies need to narrow gaps in opportunities between wealthy and poor members of their populations, as well as between members of their upper and lower social classes. These measures are necessary if we are to reduce the widespread alienation found in modern industrial societies, and if we are to encourage the collective development of creative and imaginative solutions to wide ranges of destructive social problems.

Social intelligence does not require us to have these views of the qualities of our lives in societies, but rather the education we get through developing our social intelligence often prompts us to see our societies and the world in these ways. For example, the breadth of vision that we develop directly from examining the power and complexities of the five major social influences of families, beliefs, social classes, cultures, and societies, makes us more aware and more willing to address the many social issues and social problems that result from social inequities. Increasing our social intelligence makes us more likely to use values like equality, inclusiveness, diversity, cooperation, and openness to establish a wider common good and more viable social justice in our societies.

In the same way that our social intelligence depends on our beliefs, our societies depend on our beliefs. Furthermore, the common good in our societies develops from our beliefs, with the result that social justice is also driven by our beliefs. For example, we must believe that better futures are possible, and that we can create better futures, before better futures can come into being. Although believing in these possibilities is not the whole story of becoming responsible historical actors or achieving goals that increase the common good and social justice, our beliefs are preconditions for understanding that constructive changes are possible, as well as in the long term interests of all members of our societies.

Therefore, our societies ultimately result largely from having or not having constructive beliefs about societies, as well as from our shared political will to bring about necessary changes in how we go about doing things in our daily lives. We need not only deliberately cultivate constructive beliefs about our societies, but also cooperate with others to bring our beliefs to fruition. In these respects we design and focus on visions for better futures, as well as collect social facts to monitor our progress toward goals which express the common good and social justice. Thus, our positive beliefs about the common good, social justice, and shared futures pave the way for constructive actions.

Some of the practical pointers we need to consider, when making our visions of better futures real, flow from examining our beliefs about families, social classes, cultures, and societies. Also, because our societies are multifaceted, we need to recognize and change our beliefs when necessary amidst these ongoing major social influences. Social intelligence is particularly valuable because it guides us to select beliefs to live by that increase the common good and social justice.

Social Justice and Social Classes

Social justice issues are inextricably tied to the structures of social classes in both traditional and modern societies. For example, when social classes are closed social systems, with virtually no opportunities or possibilities for upward social mobility, their societies have relatively little social justice. When social classes are open social systems, with widespread opportunities or possibilities for upward social mobility, their societies often have more social justice.

In significant respects, societies with clearly marked social classes characteristically have exclusionary consequences for many members of their populations. This means that social injustices often pervade societies, unless deliberate efforts are made to develop alternative ways for these societies to organize themselves. Even in societies where there is considerable social mobility, widespread beliefs in the importance of social classes perpetuate the existence of social classes based on arbitrary social class differences.

One of the clearest ways in which our societies demonstrate social injustices is through the arbitrariness and restrictiveness of social classes. We see, for example, that social opportunities and access to societal resources— especially material goods, education, and power—are limited by our social classes, with members of upper social classes having distinctly more goods, education, and power than members of lower social classes. Furthermore, even when modern industrial societies declare that distributions of opportunities in their populations create robust patterns in upward social mobility, generally speaking less upward social mobility is found in these societies than members of their upper social classes claim.

Social class distributions of social assets and opportunities are therefore not insignificant in restricting qualities of life in societies, often because those structures and processes that sustain social classes are supported by widespread value choices among populations. For example, social classes persist because members of societies believe that we need social classes to order our everyday lives and patterns of production or consumption. Thus entire populations reinforce social class systems because they are convinced that this is the only way to achieve the consensus and harmony necessary to keep our societies functioning well in globalization.

Populations in modern industrial societies often think that our old ways of doing things are automatically improved by mass education, and that we merely need social policies that maintain and improve access to traditional forms of education. However, social intelligence shows us that in addition to increasing the outreach and quality of mass education, societies must minimize injustices in disadvantaged social classes. For example, population members benefit from deliberately planned innovations that support the relatively new priorities of social justice. Making value choices and priority decisions to support equality, inclusiveness, diversity, cooperation, and openness increases the common good and social justice, as well as reduces social class inequalities.

Social intelligence suggests that societies are stronger in the long run, and serve the needs of their whole populations better when they reduce gaps between the advantages and disadvantages of upper and lower social classes. Designing alternative ways to organize our populations accomplishes these changes, as well as implementing policies that focus on decreasing extreme differences between the life-chances of members of upper and lower social classes. Social intelligence heightens our awareness of these possibilities, and increases the likelihood that individuals and groups achieve social justice goals.

Social classes persist in our societies because they are upheld not only by our beliefs in the importance of social classes, but also by widespread cultures and social class cultures. Social classes are so embedded in our societies that societies' values may be considered as products of their social class systems. Although beliefs in the rightness or naturalness of social classes may not be expressed explicitly in our societies' cultures, each social class tends to build social class cultures that support the vested interests of upper social class members. Therefore, social intelligence directs us to pay attention not only to the contrasts in the life experiences of members of different social classes, but also to the many ways in which social class cultures reinforce the legitimacy of our existing social classes and their injustices.

In order to develop effective multifaceted approaches to designing and implementing alternatives to social classes that make real differences in the overall organization of our societies, we need to be motivated by social justice ideals. For example, social justice strengthens our motivations to reform or remove social classes, so that we persist in our efforts in spite of populations' resistance to changing their social classes—especially the powerful opposition of members of privileged social classes who have vested interests in maintaining the status quo of unequal and unfair social classes.

When we increase our social intelligence sufficiently to aim collective actions toward achieving social justice concerns about social classes, we maintain our commitments and intentions by acting on the principles of social intelligence, the common good, and social justice. Although our ideas may have to be adjusted as we work with others, we gradually become more effective in redesigning social class practices, as well as in creating strategies to achieve social justice.

Social Justice and Cultures

Cultures are complex and powerful moving forces in our societies' histories. Cultural values support or change our societal priorities and lifestyles, for example, as during the spread of Protestantism, industrialization, and modernization. Consequently, as a result of major historical transitions, whole societies reorganize their goals through cultures. In fact, the groundswell of our cultures has the potential to bring about qualitative historical changes that may prove to be largely irreversible.

The cultural ideal of social justice is significant in relation to certain aspects of societies' changes, including new legislation to secure the rights of women, or minority groups' rights. However, because social justice values are frequently spurned, competing social systems—such as capitalism—may take hold of our cultures and societies.

Because of the relatively rapid rate of societal changes in contemporary times, it is imperative to reawaken societies' cultural and practical interests in social justice, in order to bring about social changes that reorganize societies' established ways of doing things. We cannot count on having better futures, for example, unless we tackle serious social issues—such as poverty—more directly in the present. Furthermore, we cannot deal effectively with the destructive social consequences of social classes, unless we honor alternative social justice goals and procedures.

Cultures are our most powerful avenues of social changes in our societies. However, legal systems and religions are integral parts of our cultures that keep our social classes in place, and therefore reinforce existing social inequalities. Nevertheless, when we make widespread changes in our cultures—such as through mass education—we at the same time adjust our social priorities and our usual ways of accomplishing basic societal goals. For example, education loosens the hold of traditions in cultures and societies, which historically sustained our social class differences. Consequently, educating people in all social classes increases social mobility among social classes, as well as people's interest in social justice and the likelihood that members of these societies will design effective alternatives to existing social classes.

IX. Social Justice

Thus, our cultures can promote social changes that increase social justice in and among our societies. For example, embracing relatively new or unused values in our societies—such as equality, inclusiveness, diversity, cooperation, and openness—gradually leads us toward social justice. In addition, social intelligence—a social value in its own right—directs us to formulate effective strategies to accomplish social justice goals.

It is against such a backdrop of broad cultural changes in our societies that we can assess the many ways in which social class differences based on gender, race, and ethnicity have become less restrictive. We recognize more equal relationships in our societies, for example, because we value gender, race, and ethnicity differently now. For example, when we place a higher value on all genders, races, and ethnicities, our attitudes and behavior are more focused on improving the common good and social justice for future as well as present societies.

Addressing the needs of future societies requires that we view history differently. We no longer look back through time in order to value the past, but rather decide to value the present, so that we can transform our futures by changing how we do things now. Even though we need a clear sense of history, in order to be effective historical actors in the present, we must live fully in the present so that we are sufficiently alert to create our preferred societies now for the future.

Social intelligence guides us in these endeavors, so that we continue to move forward to constructive futures. We use social intelligence as we go toward the future, in order to balance our time perspectives. For example, we look to the past largely to understand what not to repeat, rather than to idealize the past as a standard for what our present and future societies should be.

Social intelligence hones our skills as historical actors, so that societies benefit from the historical awareness that social intelligence brings to bear on the present for the future. Consequently, when we use our cultures to take a reading on current trends, for example, we are more effective in bringing about cultural and social changes that transform our societies in directions of social justice.

Historical Actors and Social Justice

An important aspect of considering the usefulness of social intelligence for resolving social issues and social problems in our societies, as well as for enhancing the qualities of our lives, is to understand how social justice promises us more constructive ways for societies and globalization to function in the modern world. As we become better educated, for example, social intelligence helps us to recognize and deal with social facts in our day-to-day business. At the same time we realize that we need to go forward decisively with others, if we are to survive and surmount the increased social stresses of globalization, especially those from technology and unplanned encounters with diverse cultures.

Because of widespread urbanization and increased access to relatively inexpensive travel facilities, we are not as isolated as we used to be historically. This means that we must develop successful strategies for living in close quarters with others if we are to survive and thrive. However, we often need to travel long distances to keep in touch with our families, for example, or to work for adequate remuneration. Although long distance relationships can make us stronger in some respects, we may also become more vulnerable to hazards through our stretched communications, increased responsibilities, and risky social situations.

Social intelligence helps us to make meaningful exchanges with others through the five major social influences of families, beliefs, social classes, cultures, and societies. Because our societies result from the power and complexities of our families, beliefs, social classes, and cultures, we see

172

that shifts within and among these strong social influences may potentially transform our societies. Also, because social intelligence prepares us to be responsible historical actors, societies can be changed substantially through leadership and democratic social movements that are inspired by social intelligence, the common good, and social justice.

Becoming an historical actor is a lifetime process. As human beings we necessarily impact history, but it is only with a much-sharpened socially intelligent awareness that we coordinate our commitments to others through actions that increase social justice. For example, we are deliberate in our decision-making as historical actors when we select values we prefer to have in our societies, and accomplish goals that mean the most to us and our societies.

In the best of all worlds our societies improve their ways of doing things when sufficient members of their populations strive to increase the common good and social justice. By contrast, widespread social forces such as capitalism expressly do not take societies' long range goals into account seriously, or encourage citizens to make long term commitments to accomplish goals that increase the common good and social justice.

Social justice is important to historical actors because it provides substance and direction for collective efforts to increase social intelligence in societies, as well as for particular goals to be accomplished in the long run. Without the breadth of vision that social intelligence, the common good, and social justice bring to bear on the decision-making and commitments of historical actors, social intelligence could not be used and expressed as effectively. The goals of social justice elevate and motivate our efforts to be responsible historical actors, so that qualitative social changes are accomplished in our societies.

However, social intelligence is not based solely on achieving social justice. For example, we may decide to become more socially intelligent in order to live more fully. This includes recognizing the needs of others—members of our families as well as members of diverse populations—as a significant aspect of being socially intelligent. We serve others in order to survive and live meaningfully, and we are responsible in our actions because we are mature adults.

Consequently, we may turn toward social justice when we are aware and responsible historical actors, in order to increase the meaning of our daily missions. We see that it is worthwhile—for pragmatic reasons as much as for moral reasons—to achieve long range goals that meet others' needs, in order to enhance the overall qualities of our lives in societies and civilizations. We also pursue equality, inclusiveness, diversity, cooperation, and openness so that we save planet earth rather than achieve conventional worldly success. These actions confirm at least a likelihood that we will survive and be fulfilled as historical actors.

Changing Societies

X. Responsibilities as Historical Actors

Social intelligence teaches us that we have responsibilities to choose how we act as we become mature adults. We realize, for example, that in part it is because of ourselves that we have created our worlds, so we need to learn how things are in order to assume more control over our destinies during our lifetimes and beyond.

Social intelligence provides this know-how because it reflects and represents major social influences in societies. Ideally, we increase our social intelligence as we grow to maturity by recognizing and expressing particular aspects of societies' major social influences that help us to achieve our preferred social conditions for all.

Social intelligence emphasizes that as adults we benefit from being thoughtful participants in organizing our societies, because this helps us to meet people's real needs rather than the wants of elites. For example, only when we aim to distribute goods, knowledge, and opportunities to all members of societies, can we achieve societies that are relatively equal, inclusive, diverse, cooperative, and open. Furthermore, if we choose to continue to perpetuate social injustices, we necessarily increase destructive influences in our societies, which inevitably lead toward the demise of our civilizations.

In these respects, social intelligence not only points out our responsibilities as historical actors, but also the pernicious consequences of actions which are not enlightened by social intelligence, the common good, or social justice. We lose what little control we have over our destinies, for example, when we do not deliberately cultivate our capacities to change the course of history by creating better societies. In fact, we not only have to face up to our responsibilities as historical actors, by making constructive choices of values and actions, but we also need to encourage others to follow suit.

As we increase our social intelligence, we see more clearly how each of us is linked directly to history and historical influences. We understand that our individual destinies are inextricably related to others' well-being, particularly to those who are members of our families, communities, and societies. Moreover, our societies should not be taken for granted, even though they frequently set the terms of our shared historical conditions, and develop either constructive or destructive situations for us to deal with as we live through time with our families and communities.

Social intelligence strengthens our appreciation of our societies and our vital connections to our societies. For example, we realize that we are existentially related to significant others in our families, local communities, whole societies, and the international community, and that nothing we do can negate or neutralize this social fact. Even when we try to isolate ourselves from others, our complex relationships to them persist.

Social intelligence shows us that our social connections do not necessarily lead to desperate social measures or unfavorable social outcomes, but rather that we benefit a great deal from developing historical relationships with members of our families, local communities, societies, and the world community. We become truly human when we honor these connections, because they make us more inclined to increase our social intelligence, pursue the common good, and unite with others to achieve social justice in our societies and the world community.

178

X. Responsibilities as Historical Actors

Even though we may not appear to be immediately successful in our endeavors to increase social justice, as long as we move in this direction, we make distinctive constructive differences to our social situations. For example, we learn how to act responsibly as historical actors in our families, as well as in relation to our beliefs, social classes, cultures, and societies. We also learn what it means to assume responsibilities to change societies as historical actors.

However, we are easily distracted from these responsibilities in modern societies. For instance, responsibility has become a taboo topic for many members of our younger generations, rather than a rallying cry to take constructive action. We need to consider these issues in deciding what our responsibilities are amidst our complex and powerful societies. We ponder questions such as can we afford to be irresponsible? What are the consequences of becoming hedonistic rather than assuming responsibilities for the fates of all members of our populations? Can we really enjoy living off the spoils of our individual and collective victories, rather than facing social realities because we are responsible for the qualities of life for all?

Although we need not be moralistic about the motives and consequences of our actions, we must be practical. Social intelligence teaches us how to be practical in our intentions to help our societies to be more independent, as well as more creative in meeting the needs of all. Living our lives fully is a practical way to assume our responsibilities as historical actors, so that we create the most productive and most just societies we can in today's unjust world.

Historical Actors in Our Families

In order to be historical actors in our societies, we must first learn how to assume responsibilities as historical actors in our families, through our beliefs, in relation to our social classes, and according to our cultural value choices.

Heightening our awareness of our social intelligence through examining our interactions with others in our families, beliefs, social classes, cultures, and societies creates foundations for understanding ourselves and the world as responsible historical actors. When we act from these socially intelligent bases as historical actors, we bring more socially intelligent awareness to bear on our decisions about which goals to choose as missions to accomplish the common good and social justice.

Our families and responsibilities in our families are the most basic building blocks of our socially intelligent being and actions. We cannot be strong and effective family members, for example, without first paying attention to the social facts of our situations in our families, and then by using social intelligence to understand and act on these facts. In order to carve out the freedom necessary to think our way into more socially intelligent actions in our families, we need to assess to what extent our families deepen our understanding of important social realities, or impede our mature grasp of social facts in our families and societies.

We are more aware historical actors in our families when we recognize repeated patterns of dominance in our families, and recall how we interacted in our families as children. Social intelligence helps us to see the many ways in which we may have been coerced into conformity, in order to maintain family harmony, or meet relatives' expectations. For example, we remember how we gave up our freedom as individuals, in order to stay loyal to the dictates of our most dominant family members. We recall the family pressures that relatives brought to bear in significant areas of their self-interest like religion or education.

One of the major goals of becoming socially intelligent, and of assuming responsibilities as historical actors, is to broaden the social perspectives we use to understand our families. As a consequence, we see ourselves more objectively in relation to our actions, rather than in static ways such as being an obedient child or grandchild. We begin to think more deeply about being selves who are thoughtful and reasonable agents, who need to make enlightened choices as responsible historical actors.

The pressures that our family members expressed to influence our thinking and actions in the past, which often continue to the present, were usually emotionally intense. Because our family interdependencies are intrinsically emotional, immature family members may try to achieve or maintain family unity and family togetherness through controlling their relationships with us. However, these patterns of contrived closeness tighten up our families' emotional systems, so that individual family members are trapped in unproductive ruts of repeated oppressive behavior, rather than free to choose among many available options to act as responsible historical actors.

We undo some of our own entrapments in the emotional intensities of our families when we are more objective about social conditions in our families, communities, and societies. We see the extent to which our families and societies need us to conform, for example, and then deliberately work to free ourselves from their expectations. By so doing we change not only our own responses to our families, but our families themselves. When we are freer agents in our families through increasing our social intelligence, we indirectly free other family members to be more independent both within and outside our families.

Thus becoming more socially intelligent is a necessary step to becoming more historically aware in our families, communities, and societies. We benefit from seeing the extent to which we are in control—or not in control—in our most intense family interactions, and in the commitments we make to our families, communities, and societies.

We do what we can to meet the needs of our relatives, especially those who are dependent on other family members, and we think more deeply about what it is we want to accomplish in our societies and lifetimes. Becoming more socially intelligent helps us to reach these goals, so that we go forward as more responsible historical actors.

Historical Actors in Our Beliefs

Our beliefs have strong influences over our behavior because they motivate us and propel us into action. For this reason, we need to be sure to review exactly what it is that we believe, and how our beliefs impact our behavior. A reliable strategy to become more objective and more critical about our beliefs is to be socially intelligent about who we are and what we want to accomplish. This is a crucial step to take because we need to cherish who we are, and what we accomplish depends on how we interact with our families, beliefs, social classes, cultures, and societies.

We become more aware historical actors through examining our beliefs as we become more socially intelligent. By contrast, if we continue to take our families' or our societies' beliefs for granted, without questioning or reassessing our priorities, we gradually lose a critical dimension of control over our beliefs, so that we cannot develop adequate senses of purpose, meaning, and direction about what we do.

Some of our most significant beliefs, that influence the qualities of our interactions with others, are how we orient ourselves to us, others, and the world. For example, are we active or passive in our inclinations to act? Do we consider our given situations and priorities thoughtfully before we act? Are we aware of the power of our beliefs in accomplishing those goals we cherish the most? Do our beliefs launch us into the world in effective ways, or do they hold us back from acting with verve and purpose?

X. Responsibilities as Historical Actors

We need to consider these vital aspects of our beliefs as carefully as possible before deciding which goals we want to accomplish in our lives, as well as how we will accomplish them. Furthermore, we need to check and recheck from time to time whether or not our beliefs serve us well, so that we can choose alternative beliefs if this is not so.

Understanding the social sources of our beliefs is an effective way to edit and reorganize our beliefs, so that we let go of beliefs that do not serve us well. Social intelligence guides us to examine our beliefs more objectively by reviewing our families, social classes, cultures, and societies as significant social sources of our beliefs. When we know what our present beliefs are, we assess more effectively which beliefs we want to eliminate or decrease, in order to develop our free agency and responsibility.

This process of reviewing, discarding, and replacing our beliefs may be long and arduous, in part because we increase our social intelligence through trial and error, depending on the particular situations we deal with each day. For example, we may need to let go of our family prejudices against college education in order to advance ourselves in our occupations or professions. In this situation, we strengthen our studies by adding beliefs that help us to discipline our work and become more productive. Furthermore, believing deeply in the goals we want to attain motivates us to persist in our endeavors, in spite of our own resistance or our relatives' opposition to our efforts to attain new professional goals.

After we change our beliefs sufficiently to free ourselves from limiting family and social commitments, we speculate objectively about opportunities and cultivate beliefs which lead us more directly to accomplish our preferred goals. At this crucial stage of developing and increasing our social intelligence, we continue to see the broader pictures of our lives, where we are historical actors who make real differences

183

in our societies. These socially intelligent perspectives help us to understand the substance of our goals more fully, as well as the means we need to attain our goals.

Our ultimate successes in achieving our preferred goals—which increase our social intelligence, the common good, and social justice—depend on our socially intelligent awareness and willingness to make new social commitments. As responsible actors we see what future societies could be like, for example, especially those that distribute the common good according to equality, inclusiveness, diversity, cooperation, and openness. We use our social intelligence and our beliefs to meet these meaningful social needs, and we work effectively with like-minded others to accomplish goals which increase social justice for all.

Historical Actors in Our Social Classes

When we become more aware of our social intelligence, and use social intelligence to assess our given situations, we see that one of the destructive qualities of social classes is that members of lower social classes are restricted from enjoying many of societies' rewards. While members of upper social classes benefit from opportunities to live fully, which sustain or increase their social class standing, the rest of the population is usually systematically deprived of such advantages. These contrasts between upper and lower social class situations mean that social classes are intrinsically restrictive and unjust to large proportions of societies and populations.

Our beliefs in social classes, as well as our social class cultures, frequently hold us back in our endeavors to increase our social intelligence, become responsible historical actors, and change social class injustices. For example, if we set out to change our social classes and societies, we are not able to accomplish this effectively without seriously considering what our existing societies are, and what alternative ways of organizing our societies could be. In order to design successful alternative ways for societies to organize themselves, we need to examine both our given social class situations and our objectives to create relatively classless societies.

An important means of defining our responsibilities as historical actors is to understand our existing social classes, as well as how these social classes influence our societies and their members' lives. For example, we start by challenging traditional ideas such as whether or not social classes are necessary for societies to exist.

We assess the usefulness of social classes by asking basic questions about what social classes do. For example, to what extent do social classes liberate members' possibilities for accomplishments, or regulate their access to opportunities, so that social classes merely reproduce themselves from generation to generation? How do social classes hold their members in place in societies by restricting their social mobility, or provide increased options for their members? How do opportunities for members of upper and lower social classes differ? Are social classes necessary for societies' social well-being? Can we survive without social classes, or with specially designed alternatives to social classes?

Because being aware, responsible historical actors is built on having adequate bases of social intelligence, we assess our specific responsibilities as historical actors by considering our actions and goals in relation to broad social influences. For example, we consider social classes in terms of their being either traditional or modern, and whether they are based on economic resources, social connections, race, ethnicity, gender, sexual orientation, occupation, or education. Thus we use social intelligence to understand the many nuances that are found in both traditional and modern social classes.

One of the outcomes of our careful assessments of social classes is that we realize more of the destructive aspects of social classes, and recognize that the benefits of members of upper classes depend on restricting the privileges of members of lower social classes. In this respect, responsible historical actors may conclude that given the difficulties and complexities of current social classes, we would thrive better from organizing societies to be more equal, inclusive, diverse, cooperative, and open. For example, we may design more advantageous alternatives to social classes by focusing on achieving social justice.

Responsible historical actors use social justice to guide their actions in replacing existing social classes with alternative ways to organize our societies. For example, responsible historical actors modify and aim to gradually eliminate extremes between privileged and underprivileged social classes, as well as social classes themselves.

Social justice goals heighten the effectiveness of responsible historical actors, so that societies become freer both within and among themselves. Furthermore, these new forms of society are not morally superior or utopian, but rather pragmatic for supporting populations in the long run, especially during times of rapid social changes and globalization.

In the meantime, before responsible historical actors can achieve these changes in social classes by working collectively with others, they must ensure that their decisions and actions are not unduly influenced by social classes, or by distributions of privileges according to social class hierarchies. Because responsible historical actors understand the value of social intelligence, they continue to refine how they are motivated, and pursue their goals to change the impacts of social classes in their own lives with clarity and verve.

Historical Actors in Our Cultures

Our cultures are important sites of productive innovations that can change our societies for the better. When we need new ideas, or new definitions of possibilities for future societies, we turn to cultural resources for inspiration. Vital cultural reserves include social ideals, knowledge, religions, laws, customs, traditions, norms, standards, and expectations. Furthermore, being responsible historical actors in cultures means that we use social intelligence, the common good, and social justice as value choices to guide our decisions and actions to create better societies for our present and futures.

Our cultures inspire us because they motivate us to act, as well as orient our actions toward accomplishing our preferred goals. For example, we use social intelligence to discover which value choices serve our needs best in proceeding toward changing our societies. As responsible historical actors we aim to achieve social justice in our societies in the long run. For example, we do what we can to establish equality, through making value choices that reflect inclusiveness, diversity, cooperation, and openness. These strategies create better societies for all to enjoy now and in the future.

Some aspects of our cultures inevitably slow down our efforts to change our societies, however well-intentioned they may be, so responsible actors need to be particularly vigilant in their value choices. For example, many individuals see virtue in returning to the past, rather than in establishing new societies. However, when we select values from past cultural and social traditions, we essentially close our minds to possibilities for establishing new ideals in future societies that increase social justice. For example, we cannot use the cultural ideals of social hierarchy or patriarchal authority in our exchanges with others if we are to create new customs of equality and inclusiveness.

Cultures are found everywhere in our societies, and they affect all members of societies. When we pay attention to the content of our cultures, we retain some control over them, because distinguishing between constructive and destructive cultural consequences moves us beyond denying these significant differences. Recognizing contrasts in cultural consequences helps us to be more responsible historical actors, and improves our collaboration in designing new cultures and new societies. Thus we no longer merely catch up with recent developments in our already established cultures.

Responsible historical actors are aware of these possibilities and conditions in our cultures. They are vigilant about the power of our consumer cultures, for example, which developed and grew during the Western industrial revolution. Even though the primary moving force of globalization is the increasingly single world economy based on capitalist market forces, we cannot afford to accept the dominance of consumer values for both our present and future societies. In order to meet the needs of entire populations, we must cultivate values and value choices that educate members of societies about their real long term interests, rather than persuade them to buy goods that merely increase the profits of major corporations.

We need cultures that support our individual and collective freedom to choose to live fully by meeting the needs of all members of our populations. Because our societies of tomorrow depend on how the content of our cultures makes survival and fulfillment possible, we must actively oversee which values we choose to nurture, in order to achieve our goals. We use social intelligence to establish and maintain our freedom, for example, so that our choices are more enlightened by addressing the needs of whole societies.

Our societies result from our cultures, and we gain control of our societies through making deliberate value choices within our cultures. When we select cultural ideals, we define directions for our societies, and exercise some control over the social consequences of our cultures. When we choose cultural priorities freely to guide our social actions, we know that our future societies will reflect our cultural ideals to some extent. In these respects, social intelligence leads us to increase the common good and social justice.

Choosing our cultures brings more constructive social realities into existence, as well as produces our present and future societies. We have the social problems we have in large part because of our cultures, which means that we can change some of the most pernicious social consequences of our problems by changing our cultures. We regain control over our cultures by producing the cultures we prefer, which consequently create those societies we really choose.

Historical Actors in Our Societies

Social intelligence helps us to maintain a broad social awareness of our societies as well as of ourselves. For example, when we are socially intelligent we see ourselves not only as family members or individuals with commitments based on beliefs, but also as participants in social classes and cultures. As we continue to increase our social intelligence we eventually strengthen our understanding of history sufficiently to have a marked sense of history, and we respond to the changing times of history as members of our societies. This gradual building of our awareness of being members of our societies, through increasing our social intelligence, strengthens our identities as historical actors.

Socially intelligent historical actors are responsible because they understand the social consequences of their actions, and strive to construct better societies today for the future. One strategy for pursuing and accomplishing these goals is to consider what the common good of our societies is or could be, so that we meet objectives related to increasing the common good and the well-being of all.

Social intelligence teaches us that actively considering and meeting needs that represent the well-being of all is a necessary condition for the survival and fulfillment of individual members of our societies. When groups are disadvantaged, the deep satisfactions of members of advantaged groups are impaired, because we are not responsible members of societies when we knowingly live at the expense of others.

In the long run societies have more vested interests in socially intelligent historical actors than in members of their populations who are committed to maintaining a status quo of privileges for a few and disadvantages for most. Because people who are disadvantaged often ultimately react negatively to inequalities, we jeopardize the security of our societies when we live in unjust social conditions. Social intelligence is pragmatic in assessing the long term ineffectiveness of some of our well-established social institutions, such as social classes, and encourages historical actors to design alternative social realities of equality, inclusiveness, diversity, cooperation, and openness.

Ultimately historical actors consider the priorities of equality, inclusiveness, diversity, cooperation, and openness in each of their actions, to ensure that they move toward social justice rather than social destruction. Furthermore, socially intelligent historical actors are motivated to accomplish goals which benefit all, rather than goals which serve the needs of elites. Although every member of our societies is an historical actor, because each one of us impacts the histories of our societies whether we realize this or not, those who are socially intelligent historical actors are more aware and more responsible, so they are more constructive in their impacts on whole societies.

Modern societies often try to establish universal education to serve the needs of their entire populations. They understand that the well-being of their societies derives from the level of enlightenment—or ignorance—of all members of their populations. Even though many different qualities of education may be available to members of modern societies, in the long run it is societies whose whole populations receive the best educations that achieve the most life satisfaction, as well as needed goods and services. This approach to designing education is socially intelligent, and creates better societies in the present for the future.

Even though our social intelligence is firmly rooted in our families' experiences, it must also be rooted in our societies to some extent. We have to appreciate the power and complexities of our societies, for example, so that we are not content to cultivate blind patriotism rather than empathy. Thus we do not unite with our societies' values in order to take sides in relation to other societies, but rather to increase our awareness and understanding of globalization and the international societies that surround us and permeate our everyday exchanges.

In recent years, the world has become a smaller place, due to advances in technology and increased travel. Even though our loyalties to our own societies may continue to be strong, we need to develop an historical awareness that each of our societies is linked to a world system of societies in distinctive ways. For example, we have social classes within our societies and between or among our societies. Consequently, our own societies have social standing among the world-wide statuses of different societies. Therefore, as historical actors we must know as much as we can about global connections among societies, in order to act responsibly.

Responsible Changes in Societies

Social intelligence suggests that we are responsible when we aim to change societies, to the extent that we exercise caution in promoting and implementing our innovations. This enables us to prevent or minimize any destructive consequences that may flow from our actions. Thus, responsible historical actors need to be sufficiently knowledgeable about societies and social influences to predict the consequences of their proposed actions fairly accurately before they act. In these respects, responsible historical actors follow strategies to change societies only when they are reasonably sure that constructive outcomes will result from their actions.

Social intelligence helps us to meet this stringent standard of responsibility in becoming historical actors. Even though mistakes are inevitably made, when we orient our lives toward living as historical actors, we habitually anticipate the outcomes of our actions as accurately as possible before we develop alternatives to the status quo. For example, we collect and interpret social facts, such as trend data or knowledge about the experiences of other societies, which show us how to increase our effectiveness in innovating in our societies. Social intelligence also points out that we increase our skills in changing societies when we act collectively with others.

Responsible changes in societies include a wide range of social innovations, from measures intended to limit the destructiveness of others' ongoing actions, to designing innovations which reorganize our societies. For example, responsible historical actors may build on their experiences and knowledge of families to implement political policies that meet the needs of all families, especially disadvantaged families. Social intelligence also informs historical actors about ways to initiate changes in existing social classes, so that more people gain freedom to choose how to live rather than support traditional social class restrictions on identities and goals through different generations.

Social intelligence encourages the development of specific orientations for taking actions to change societies as historical actors, such as working toward increasing the common good or social justice. In these respects, working with likeminded others becomes easier, and cooperative actions are more effective.

X. Responsibilities as Historical Actors

Therefore, social ideals such as the common good and social justice are practical goals or ends for historical actors' innovative actions to change societies. These ideals strengthen historical actors' motivations, as well as encourage persistence in spite of disappointments or others' resistance, that often impede the accomplishment of goals to change societies.

Responsible changes in societies follow democratic principles because, in spite of their many problems, democracies have proved themselves to be more socially intelligent than other political regimes in the long run. For example, the masses in modern or traditional societies are represented more equally in collective democratic decisions. Although particular democratic policies or initiatives frequently compete with each other, most democratic legislation applies equally to all members of societies. Furthermore, addressing common good and social justice concerns enhances democratic policies, because they ensure that there is sufficient widespread acknowledgement that societies' long term survival and fulfillment needs must be met.

Thus democratic principles guide historical actors' agendas for changing societies through establishing new laws, which are incorporated into existing legal systems and established ways of doing things. In these respects, historical actors' efforts to make responsible changes in societies do not necessarily shake up the status quo, but rather remake or reform ways to accomplish shared ends such as the common good and social justice.

Although accomplishing slow, gradual changes in societies is not the only route that responsible historical actors follow in changing societies, historical actors do not deny the value of accommodating to some established ways of doing things. However, the principles of both social intelligence and democracies forbid historical actors to coerce others to conform to innovations that do not meet their basic needs and preferences.

Because historical actors are most responsible and effective in bringing about constructive changes in societies when they understand the social realities of societies, and make deliberate value choices to create societies that meet long term needs for the future, we will examine social realities in societies next, and then look at how to choose societies that we really want in the future. The following two chapters of *Societies and Social Intelligence* show us how to recognize and deal with social realities, and how to choose societies that nurture and sustain us in the long run, in spite of the powerful social pressures of vested interests and globalization to maintain the status quo.

XI. Social Realities and Societies

A recurring theme of *Societies and Social Intelligence* is that social intelligence derives from at least five strong social influences in our societies. We need to consider these influences carefully in relation to our thinking and actions, if we are to be socially intelligent, and if we are concerned about how we and other people can survive and thrive in today's globalization and the future.

All five of these strong social influences are social realities in their own right, because they have significant positive or negative impacts on what we imagine we can do and what we actually do. For example, they are powerful social realities because they generate social facts that essentially define who we are, how we relate to other people, our world views, what we want to accomplish, and what we actually accomplish.

We become more socially intelligent when we examine and understand more fully the power of these social realities in our everyday lives, as well as their impacts on our national and international policies. For example, we understand ourselves and our goals better when we have a solid working knowledge about what to expect from our families, beliefs, social classes, cultures, and societies. Thus, being socially intelligent requires us to give priority to planning our daily strategies to survive and accomplish our aims in life by seriously considering the social realities and social influences of families, beliefs, social classes, cultures, and societies.

We use the broad socially intelligent perspective of societies in order to deliberately cultivate our social intelligence. For example, we understand more fully that societies cannot survive or thrive without the basic social conditions and social realities of families, beliefs, social classes, and cultures. Furthermore, we realize that these social realities of societies define significant qualities of globalization.

Our societies are held together because of the mutually beneficial and even the destructive social realities of our families, beliefs, social classes, and cultures. In fact, our societies can only continue to perpetuate themselves and reach their most cherished goals when their families, beliefs, social classes, and cultures are reasonably well-coordinated. Moreover, the degree of integration of social realities in societies also defines significant aspects of globalization.

Because our families, beliefs, social classes, cultures, and societies play fundamentally important roles in our collective lives, as well as in our personal lives, we need to be aware of how these social realities and strong social influences operate. For example, we acknowledge the social realities of families, beliefs, social classes, cultures, and societies because they affect each of us in deep-seated, emotional ways. Furthermore, we benefit from becoming more socially intelligent when we interact with these five social realities to accomplish social justice. However, we also suffer marked negative consequences from these social realities to the extent that we choose to ignore their power and complexities.

Even if we choose to ignore the social realities of families, beliefs, social classes, cultures, and societies, globalization happens. Globalization has gathered sufficient momentum during modern times that societies' forces predictably proceed in this direction, whether or not we choose to participate actively in the social realities of our societies.

In many powerful societies the best of all worlds is to assume some responsibilities for improving the qualities of globalization, so that all societies benefit. At some level, most societies want to save themselves and the world from destructive forces, by using practical means such as social intelligence to create advantageous future social conditions for all. For example, there is still widespread hope that our shared goals of survival and fulfillment are practical rather than impossible ideals. Consequently, social intelligence encourages us to deal with social realities in our everyday lives rather than merely dream about utopias.

In order to more fully understand how our families, beliefs, social classes, cultures, and societies interact as complex social realities, we examine relationships among families, beliefs, social classes, cultures, and societies in this chapter of *Societies and Social Intelligence*. We also scrutinize these five social realities in the contexts of globalization, changing societies, and social justice. For example, we use social intelligence to guide us while relating to the social realities of families, beliefs, social classes, cultures, and societies, so that we improve globalization and future worlds by creating more just societies.

Families in Societies

When we view families from the socially intelligent perspective of societies, we see that societies are dependent on families for their existence and survival through time. Moreover, societies need families not only to produce new members of their populations, but also because families have largely proved themselves superior to other means of raising children. For example, families can orient and prepare the youngest generations of societies' populations effectively for present and future challenges.

The in-depth nurturing and training in the vast majority of families in societies, even if viewed largely as life-preserving tasks, cannot be replicated easily by other social institutions. Although societies and families need cultures to

197

support them—for example, to convince adults that families are important, or that raising children is worthwhile and enjoyable—the more important social reality is that families fill broad and deep social needs for intimacy in societies, as well as individuals' desires.

Consequently, families have political as well as personal characteristics. For example, even though we may enjoy many private satisfactions from our families, this social fact does not make the broad social and political significance of our families a less important social reality in our societies.

Social intelligence heightens our awareness of family connections and mediations between our personal lives and the foundational needs of societies. Sometimes we experience conflicts between the immediacy of our family members' particular wants—especially those concerning access to societal resources such as education—and the ongoing survival needs of our societies. Furthermore, because we are often deeply committed to our families—to both our parents' families and our new adult families—we may not readily associate the tensions and stresses we experience in our family relationships with societal pressures to meet particular standards or goals for maintaining or improving our societies.

When we understand the broader social realities of our families at the same time that we increase our social intelligence, we become freer to live more responsible lives with respect to our families. For example, we realize more fully how even the most intense personal exchanges within our families reinforce or challenge shared expectations about families and societies.

Social intelligence prompts us to consider the broad social realities of families at the same time that we continue to be emotionally invested in our families, so that we make more socially intelligent decisions about resources, beliefs, and actions. For example, we appreciate more fully that we and our families are significant social realities in our societies, as well as important means for societies' survival and well-being.

Developing broad societal perspectives on our personal lives alerts us to the power and complexities of families and genders in societies. Consequently, we consider some of the most restrictive aspects of these social realities carefully, so that we can more easily predict the resistance and pressures to conform that are evoked by particular lines of action in our families and societies.

This broad view of families and societies frees us, because we understand more clearly how the powerful undertow of families is a significant social reality in our societies. It also makes us more aware of the value and power of our individual capacities to make decisions and judgments about our goals and priorities, because we cannot afford to sacrifice our personal integrity to these broad social realities.

When we allow ourselves to be trapped by the emotional intensity of our families, or by the needs of particular family members, we lose touch with some of the broader social realities of families in societies. This detachment often leads us to over-value the personal aspects of our families, so that we may wallow endlessly in our reactions to other family members' demands, without paying attention to the importance of trying to live freely and meaningfully in our families.

Even in the most compelling emotional crises or everyday situations in our families, social intelligence helps us to be objective, so that we maintain more balance in our responsiveness to the social realities that our families are both personal and necessary social foundations of our societies' survival and prosperity. Ideally we neither allow our families to overwhelm us, nor deny our responsibilities to meet the real needs of our family members. Social intelligence does not suggest that we avoid our family responsibilities, but rather insists on the beneficial effects of considering social justice issues in relation to our families, such as making the privileges of our families more widespread in societies and globalization.

Beliefs in Societies

Beliefs in societies are important social realities which both support and resist social changes, especially changes related to established characteristics of our societies. We are born into maelstroms of contradictory beliefs, and those who are emotionally closest to us routinely encourage us to embrace particular beliefs and use them as our own. For example, we become participants in religions, or in local traditions, through our families' shared beliefs, and these beliefs largely determine our views of ourselves, others, and the world.

Beliefs during childhood are often clear and strong social realities in our everyday lives, so they are readily retained when we are adults. We become human as we absorb particular social beliefs, and we lead meaningful lives—or not—because we accept these beliefs. However, when we continue to use beliefs from our youth in our adult lives, this loyalty or faith may no longer be in our own interests. For example, we can be held back by families' archaic traditional beliefs that resist the impacts of modern societies and contemporary beliefs.

Social intelligence helps us to be critical about our beliefs and their social consequences, so that we are more authentic in choosing our own beliefs. For example, when we examine the social sources of our beliefs more closely, we can assess the inadequacies of those beliefs we take for granted as essential social realities that guide our lives. However, a true test of the usefulness of our current beliefs is the extent to which they support our needs to be fulfilled by increasing the common good or social justice.

Social intelligence encourages us to honor beliefs in societies that uphold what we want to accomplish, or how we think our societies should be. Constructive and inspiring beliefs exist, and it is our responsibility as socially intelligent human beings—or historical actors—to be selective in choosing beliefs that accomplish social justice individually and collectively. For example, we deliberately seek out more empathic or altruistic beliefs which explicitly guide us to discover ways to work with others to challenge existing beliefs in social classes or other restrictive social realities.

It is not easy to change our beliefs, or even to see nuances in the social realities of beliefs in societies. Nevertheless, observing how consumers are influenced by their beliefs in market forces illustrates some aspects of the power of the social realities of contemporary beliefs, as well as our resistance to changing our most deep-seated beliefs.

Social intelligence encourages us to be aware of the repetitiveness and thoughtlessness of some of our belief habits. Given the social reality that beliefs are important to our societies as well as to us, it behooves us to find ways to clarify and strengthen our beliefs. Social intelligence makes us bolder and braver in our everyday lives, so that we continue to challenge even our most hidden beliefs in whatever it is that we take for granted about individuals, communities, and societies.

We also heighten our awareness about the social realities of beliefs in our societies by examining how our beliefs about families reinforce or challenge varied constructive and destructive beliefs. For example, beliefs have emotional impacts on our behavior, and the intensity of these shared emotional influences often strengthens societies' resistance to modifying or accommodating social traditions and current social realities.

Collective emotional characteristics of traditional beliefs historically tend to hold societies together, but at the same time may set societies on destructive paths through their adaptations to globalization. In these respects, the social realities of beliefs are often accepted as foundations or structures of societies, when in fact they are social products that could be significantly modified through time when sufficient people cultivate more constructive beliefs and act accordingly.

Beliefs are also considered to be important social realities in societies because they support social classes in societies and globalization, as well as form the lifeblood of complex local, national, and international cultures. However, because societies result from the impacts of these different beliefs, we need to recognize and deal effectively with beliefs that do not serve our long range interests in the common good of modern societies and globalization.

Social intelligence is useful because it helps us to sort out these contradictory social realities about beliefs; it dispels collective ignorance in beliefs; and it guides us to build better future societies. Becoming more socially intelligent starts the complex process of assessing how we relate to the social realities of beliefs in our past and current societies, as well as what kinds of societies we want to create for the future.

Social Classes in Societies

Social classes are another significant social reality in societies which need to be acknowledged and dealt with in relation to our individual and collective goals to change societies. Social classes are not only an ongoing existing social reality, but also a potential social reality which can reemerge at any time, especially when there are crises or rapid social changes. For example, we tend to organize social groups through hierarchies, so that when standards of behavior or others' expectations about our actions are unclear, social classes are invoked to bring solidarity, order, and stability to this ambiguous situation.

Therefore, when we engage in social changes which increase social intelligence or social justice, we need to be ever vigilant that social classes are not perpetuated as social realities. For example, in order to make constructive social changes, we benefit from finding alternative ways to organize ourselves, so that inequalities are no longer built into how we interact and think about each other at deep-seated levels. Ideally, social intelligence is a means to change established social realities that do not increase the common good for all. When we are socially intelligent, we work collectively toward creating new constructive social realities which express social justice.

Many social class social realities are experienced as particular patterns of behavior about economic, educational, or physiological differences, as well as wide varieties of social distinctions among individuals and populations. Some of the most pervasive characteristics of social class realities are social inequalities, limited opportunities, restricted lifestyles, prejudice, and discrimination, which may be found to some extent in all our basic social institutions. Although it is not possible in the short run to dramatically modify the complex and powerful mechanisms that hold our current social classes in place, we can change how we act and how we make collective decisions about changing the most destructive characteristics of social classes.

Social intelligence helps us to recognize and understand some of the most pernicious consequences of social classes. For example, when we increase our social intelligence we appreciate the power of social classes more fully, which often inspires motivations to change social classes. Our deepened grasp of the limiting characteristics of social classes, helps us to see how changing the social realities of social classes makes relating to each other more beneficial.

Although broad social policies about education or individual legal rights may have positive impacts on reducing unjust social class privileges, we must still create additional measures to reduce the restrictiveness of social classes. For example, we make differences in our lives and others' experiences when we incorporate socially intelligent awareness about social class realities in our everyday exchanges and goals. Consequently, we change social classes indirectly as well as directly as we go about our daily business in the world at large.

Even though the history of social class realities suggests that because social classes have always existed in some form, they will inevitably perpetuate themselves in the future, social intelligence helps us to be more objective. For example, because social classes are human creations, we cannot conclude that social classes are impossible to change or modify meaningfully to benefit all members of societies. In fact, social intelligence is based on the principle that human strategies can always be changed because they are learned, and that becoming more socially intelligent is a practical way to understand how to make significant changes in our social classes.

Consequently, we recognize that it is possible to change whatever social classes we identify with, and whatever values we espouse that support current social classes. Social intelligence is a pragmatic survival and fulfillment strategy, which encourages us to learn how we can be more effective in decreasing the social injustices of social class social realities in societies.

Social intelligence guides us to build stronger societies for a future where all share the benefits of our common good. In order to achieve this goal, we learn to modify and minimize the most destructive social realities of social classes; we use new ways to organize ourselves in meaningful adaptations to globalization; and we make sure that all benefit from new local, national, and global social realities in our societies. These attitudes and actions allow us to identify and act in accordance with the social justice values of equality, inclusiveness, diversity, cooperation, and openness in achieving a more viable common good.

XI. Social Realities and Societies

Cultures in Societies

Cultures make being human possible, and societies possible. To the extent that all human beings are social, our human interdependence is necessarily expressed in our societies' cultural symbols and communications. We articulate our humanness through values and ideals which flow from our societies' cultures, so cultures are significant social realities in their own right. Cultures can also lead us in new directions when we set out to change our societies.

Societies are important social influences largely because they produce their own cultures. For example, nationalism and patriotism may have dramatically stark impacts on us, due to the social realities of nationalistic or patriotic cultural values and ideals in personal and political decisions. Thus societies need cultures in order to protect their populations effectively.

Social intelligence heightens our awareness of the importance of cultures in our societies, and the significance of cultural values and ideals in how we understand ourselves, others, societies, and the world. Being members of societies includes accepting particular cultural values and ideals: we are who we are because we express shared cultural values and ideals in our everyday behavior.

When there is insufficient acceptance of shared cultural values by individuals or groups, some members of societies are treated differently from others or sanctioned for their behavior. For example, the labels and punishments we use to express collective disapproval of deviance, crime, and treason derive from our shared senses of betrayal about societies' or cultures' strongest values and ideals.

When we grasp the power and complexities of the social realities of cultures in our lives through increasing our social intelligence, we take control over whether we continue to accept those cultural values and ideals that have guided our actions in the past, or whether we pursue different cultural values and ideals. As we increase our social intelligence, we see more clearly that if we are to have future societies that honor social justice, it is up to us to create and sustain cultures that strengthen alternative values and ideals such as equality, inclusiveness, diversity, cooperation, and openness. For example, our cultures of nationalism and patriotism must be sufficiently benign, so that our new ways to organize our societies allow us to co-exist peacefully.

When we make new value choices in order to be more socially intelligent, we create thoughtful changes in our personal lives and families. This socially intelligent process readies us to tackle some of the broad issues in the social realities of our cultures and societies. For example, we continue to assess social facts in recent historical trends in our cultures, so that we can use social intelligence principles to find like-minded others who make thoughtful commitments with us to achieve strategic cultural changes in our societies.

Becoming historical actors, through reorienting our lives to work toward increasing social justice, is often a late stage of becoming socially intelligent. For example, continuing to increase our social intelligence deepens our understanding of how to work cooperatively and effectively with likeminded others, so that we change the social realities of our national and international cultures. Social intelligence continues to guide us in assessing the broad dynamics and social realities of our cultures and societies, so that we make significant impacts by being responsible historical actors in our cultures and societies, as well as in relation to our families, beliefs, and social classes.

We achieve the objectivity and balance necessary to maintain socially intelligent perspectives in our everyday lives by responding to personal, professional, and political needs in our families, beliefs, social classes, cultures, and societies. We cannot content ourselves with looking at just a few social realities in our cultures and societies, because this inevitably gives us only partial views of what is really going on in current historical trends.

Thus we find and work on cultural social realities in our personal relationships, as well as in the social facts of our societies, contemporary history, and globalization. Staying grounded in the social realities of our cultures helps us to maintain a broad socially intelligent awareness. Social intelligence then guides us to choose cultural values and ideals that increase the common good and social justice, because we know that we want to survive and thrive by creating more constructive future societies.

Societies in Globalization

Although today's societies continue to be significant social realities for most populations, increasing rates of globalization challenge the wide variety of ways in which people organize themselves in and among our nation states. Whereas until relatively recent times nation states had marked degrees of consistency in their histories and social changes, today and in the foreseeable future societies' boundaries are increasingly in flux, especially when tensions between traditional and modern societies develop into intense political conflicts or wars.

Therefore, societies must deal with difficult questions such as how nation states achieve workable degrees of internal social solidarity at the same time that they accommodate to international social, economic, and political forces. To the extent that globalization increased in recent decades due to capitalist market forces, societies need to decide on their priorities, policies, and strategies by assessing what is most economically feasible and politically expedient in relation to both internal and external social realities.

Social intelligence requires us to understand modern societies from the standpoint of these complex internal and external social dynamics both within and outside our societies. For example, sometimes economic forces dominate other social influences within and outside our societies, whereas in different situations political stresses may precipitate social changes within and among our societies. By contrast, those societies which have successfully resisted modernization and secularization may continue to be influenced more strongly by the social realities of traditions in families, beliefs, social classes, and cultures, rather than by the social realities of economics and politics.

We need social intelligence to help us to understand and act on these broad issues and networks of special interests both within and outside our societies. Even though we may think it more relevant to examine immediate national social realities which define our families, beliefs, social classes, and cultures, we also need to maintain views of our societies as history in the making, and as integral parts of continuing globalization.

We cannot increase our social intelligence and become historical actors without sustaining our awareness of these broadest views of our societies, our lives, and our worlds. Furthermore, one of the major purposes of becoming more socially intelligent is to reflect on the global social dynamics that influence our societies, so that we see more clearly who we are and where we are going as individuals, societies, and civilizations. We must not become overwhelmed by globalization, for example, or travel internationally for recreational purposes only.

Part of becoming more aware of the social realities of our particular societies and international globalization is to explore the impacts of power as well as market forces within and outside our societies. We need to consider carefully the facts that even though both our societal economies and the world economy are powerful definers of how we live on a daily basis, their social realities and forces also have social origins, and are therefore subject to human interventions and changes.

For example, one of the reasons that capitalism has largely taken over how we organize our societies is that capitalism has its own supporting beliefs and cultures, which are changeable social creations. Similarly, the power and authority structures in societies that are based on traditions and customs are often kept alive by our families, but they too can be changed.

When we are socially intelligent we learn about the most significant social realities that underlie our societies, such as power and patterns in economic interests. When we understand these social realities sufficiently, we can bring about more enlightened and more deliberately planned social changes. For example, when we are responsible socially intelligent historical actors, we work with others to design alternative social realities, so that we do not automatically accept the dominance of existing economic and political power relations without questioning their ultimate goals and purposes.

To the extent that we are effective in finding likeminded others to assist us in our socially intelligent questioning of the status quo, we are more able to work collectively to increase the common good and social justice within and among our societies. Social intelligence principles help us to change our societies and globalization: we create new social realities that encourage us to increase the common good and social justice for all.

Changing Societies Toward Social Justice

When we understand the power and complexities of social realities in our societies more fully—which includes examining how influential social realities are connected to our families, beliefs, social classes, and cultures—we are ready to assume broader responsibilities as historical actors. Our understanding of social realities makes our actions more responsible, as well as more effective, by ultimately increasing the common good and social justice, usually through collective actions. Even though we cannot realistically expect our early efforts toward increasing social justice to have deep impacts on our societies, we can rest assured that how we think and what we do start momentums of changes in this direction.

Our knowledge of social realities that connects our families, beliefs, social classes and cultures with our societies is invaluable for grasping how our societies operate as independent societies, as well as in relation to globalization. Furthermore, these social realities are necessarily based on social facts rather than moral ideals, which ground the social intelligence principles we incorporate in our everyday lives and strategies to change societies.

Because societies' social realities are both complex and powerful, unless we are aware of them and use their power and complexities for our own purposes, they will use us. For example, we are increasingly at the mercy of established social realities in our societies when we passively allow them to maintain the status quo, or when we use them to adapt to broad social pressures rather than to respond to the needs of most people in our populations. Our social intelligence challenge is therefore to use existing social realities as starting points to discern what needs to be changed, so that we can design new social realities to create better future societies.

Thus the quality of our working knowledge of social realities tends to free or restrict our goals. For example, social realities may compel us to maintain social classes as they are in our societies today, or inspire us to design and implement alternative ways to organize ourselves. Social intelligence helps us to discern these significant differences, which enables us to invest our energies and creativity in building better societies for the future.

When we are aware historical actors we conduct ourselves responsibly by continuing to change our value choices, in the knowledge that value choices change our societies constructively through socially intelligent actions. For example, when we pursue social values like equality, inclusiveness, diversity, cooperation, and openness in our quests to design alternative ways to organize our populations, we do not merely reinforce societies' social class beliefs, cultures, or social realities.

In many respects the social realities of our families in societies continue to be foundations for our efforts to be socially intelligent, to serve as historical actors, and to accomplish social justice. Because of the significance of our emotional bonds with our families and our beliefs about the social realities of our families, we must ensure that our family connections to societies are strong and secure for innovative actions. If we do not honor our family social realities in these socially intelligent ways, we predictably reinforce restrictive conditions and limited consequences for our actions with respect to our value choices, the world, and strategies to accomplish social changes.

Social intelligence helps us to recognize social realities in our societies. Social intelligence also shows us how to assess social realities' strategic significance in guiding societies to establish and implement their best priorities. As socially intelligent beings, we harness our capacities to think and make value choices on behalf of our intended goals to create better societies for the future. We use social intelligence to deepen our understanding of the complex social pressures and social issues involved in changing societies, for example, so that we more realistically choose our preferred societies and preferred personal lives.

In these ways social intelligence awakens us to destinies we may have only dreamed of, or considered momentarily. Amidst worrying times of continuing strife and political tensions we can make more meaningful personal, professional, and political choices that allow us to work with others in socially intelligent ways toward social justice goals. Our capacities to think clearly, make judgments, and act are sufficient for our shared salvation to the extent that we understand the social realities we have to deal with, and the value choices we need to make.

XII. Choosing Societies

When we use social intelligence to guide us in changing our societies, we deliberately choose what kinds of societies we want to construct. For example, social intelligence principles make us individually and collectively aware of what we need to remove or diminish in our existing societies, so that we can avoid repeating mistakes of the past, or prevent ourselves from falling into ruts that produce the same social problems and social issues of our current societies in the future.

Starting out with socially intelligent intentions to increase the common good and social justice, we examine how we can organize our individual and collective efforts to achieve these goals in this chapter of *Societies and Social Intelligence*. Our shared priority is to honor the intrinsic power of our societies in our everyday lives and our shared destinies as human beings. When we realize that we cannot exist without our societies, our most essential question is how to make our societies truly our own, so that we and our unborn children are fulfilled.

As in other areas where we apply social intelligence to making changes in our families, beliefs, social classes, and cultures, we act with the awareness that changing our ways of thinking and being can increase the effectiveness of our strategies to improve our societies. When we clarify our goals, for example, as well as maintain the broader pictures of our lives in order to be objective, we understand the most significant social facts in our shared social conditions more deeply. This enables us to progress toward our goals to better our societies, because we make more enlightened value choices about what societies we want to create. We establish a socially intelligent vision of our preferred future societies, and make responsible decisions for the social fulfillment of all.

Although we understand that we cannot be completely successful in creating societies that bring fulfillment to all members of our populations in the short run, we need to develop aims, intentions, and goals that at least point us in this direction. As socially intelligent individuals and historical actors, we then proceed in the knowledge that whatever we decide to do to increase the common good and social justice responds constructively to our lived experiences and current social realities.

Social intelligence, the common good, and social justice may be thought of as moral ideals that keep us on track to reach our goals. However, we must also pay close attention to the ongoing detailed social facts of our social situations, as well as the extent of our real progress toward what we are accomplishing, if we want to attain a satisfactory degree of precision in meeting our goals.

Social intelligence requires us, at all stages of trying to change our societies, to continue to be objective by considering as many of our options as possible. For example, we only really choose our own better societies when we are sufficiently free to see the options available to design and formulate specific values for future societies. Furthermore, we must be ever vigilant not to react destructively to social pressures that perpetuate social classes as they are, for example, or extend existing social inequalities into the future.

Because social intelligence makes us freer, more thoughtful, more creative, and clearer in our goals, social intelligence principles can be relied on to guide us to establish more humane societies in the present for the future. For example, concentrating on meeting the real needs of all, through applying social intelligence in strategies to reduce social inequities, ensures increased fulfillment in our future societies. We also focus on making value choices that express the common good and social justice, such as equality, inclusiveness, diversity, cooperation, and openness. These strategies reinforce the effectiveness of our collective actions to improve our futures.

Even though the tools of social intelligence can be abused, like other social resources, when we become more socially intelligent we understand more fully what it takes to coexist peacefully, and what we can do to accomplish this. Part of our own fulfillment in becoming more socially intelligent consists of finding people who share our constructive goals. Although we may disagree about which socially intelligent means we need to create societies that are more socially just, working cooperatively and openly helps us to achieve our goals.

Vision

Before we take action on particular strategies to change our societies, especially when we have increased our social intelligence to become responsible historical actors, we need to assess the practicality of our social starting points in societies. For example, social intelligence enables us to answer several basic questions about societies, so that we proceed more effectively in directions that truly work toward choosing our preferred societies.

Some basic questions about our societies include social issues such as what are the most critical ways in which our families, beliefs, social classes, and cultures fall short of serving our populations' needs? What major social problems and social issues result from what we have learned about our societies? Why have we been unable to achieve sufficient social justice in our societies? What are some of the most successful social changes that have already been accomplished in our societies? How were these accomplished?

When we are more objective about the strengths and weaknesses of our societies, we can assess what our societies could or should provide for us and with us. What particular goals do our societies want to accomplish? What goals do we want our societies to accomplish? How can we achieve these goals with existing means? What do we need to expand our resources and strategies to make more changes possible? Who is sufficiently responsible and committed to see these needed changes through? How can we democratize and educate our populations so that socially intelligent leaders assume responsibilities necessary for changing our societies constructively?

Social intelligence gives us tools to state, examine, and answer these questions. For example, we realize— through applying social intelligence principles to existing social problems and social issues—that we can unlearn and redo whatever people have created. Furthermore, social intelligence is particularly useful in this endeavor, because of its practical hands-on knowledge about power, resources, and human skills.

Because we are human and social creations, we can opt to lead our lives differently by establishing new ways to accomplish new goals. Social intelligence helps us consistently in these major endeavors because it enables us to think more objectively and more broadly, as well as teaches us how to work with others cooperatively and openly.

Before we make changes that are necessary for increasing social justice in our societies, however, we must first create or design visions of how things could be in our societies, in order to motivate and inspire individual and collective actions. Even though the rewards of working with such visions are not immediate, social intelligence makes us sufficiently knowledgeable about the social conditions we want to create, that we continue to progress toward the common good and social justice. Knowing what we are doing—or trying to do—makes considerable differences in our societies, and at the same time motivates us to persist in our efforts.

Our socially intelligent focus on families, beliefs, social classes, cultures, and societies helps us to understand the deepest parts of ourselves, which include both our resistance to taking action and our strong commitments to bring constructive social changes into being. When we see where we are in our societies, know where we want to go, and acknowledge the effectiveness of socially intelligent strategies as well as the power and complexities of social realities, we are on our way to accomplish goals that increase the common good and social justice. Socially intelligent guiding perspectives deepen our understanding of individual and collective possibilities. They also clarify our visions of the particular goals we want to accomplish and the strategies we need to use.

Developing a strong sense of history helps us to get into the spirit of considering and visualizing changes in our societies. History enables us to appreciate the power of slow gradual changes in societies, for example, as well as suggests possibilities for rapid social changes. The intrinsic precariousness and unpredictability of our social situations need not be discouraging, however, because we know that we can continue to be guided by social intelligence principles. The security of moving in this general direction increases precision in our choices of how to change our societies. Thus social intelligence is critical in increasing social justice and bringing fulfillment to all members of our populations.

Precision

Precision is a means which brings our socially intelligent visions of future societies to fruition. We can both approach how to create and cultivate a vision of our chosen societies through the principles of social intelligence, and bring that vision into being as a social reality with a significant degree of precision. For practical purposes, the precision of our aims and results is necessary, to make our efforts and accomplishments effective, in applying principles of social intelligence to improving our societies.

Social intelligence gives us selective broad views of our societies through assessments of the five major social influences of families, beliefs, social classes, cultures, and societies. When we practice applying social intelligence to our everyday lives, we appreciate more fully how strongly these five social influences determine who we are, what we aspire to, and how we go about accomplishing our goals. We understand more fully how families, beliefs, social classes, cultures, and societies define basic qualities of our lives, due in large part to the emotional depth of our shared reactions to social traditions, to pressures to conform to others' expectations, and to needs to have some peace and harmony in our societies in order to get on with our lives.

Ideally we free ourselves sufficiently from these five major social influences so that we clarify our thinking about existential issues such as how dependent we are on others—for example, in our families, social classes, and societies—and to what extent we can create societies to meet the needs of all members of our populations more realistically. The principles of social intelligence guide us to maintain reliable broad views of families, beliefs, social classes, cultures, and societies, so that we are less reactive in either accepting or rejecting these social pressures. Thus, increasing our social intelligence enables us to think more clearly about populations and societies, so that we are more realistic in assessing our preferred goals, and how to create societies with a common good that is shared more justly by all.

218

XII. Choosing Societies

Our visions of better societies have more precision when they are informed by these principles of social intelligence, because then they are based on social facts. For example, we are increasingly objective when we are socially intelligent, which helps us to see and consider more social options for ourselves and others. Furthermore, understanding what the power and complexities of societies are—and have been in the past—enables us to ground our cultural ideals to improve societies through social facts. This socially intelligent strategy also increases the precision of our visions of societal change.

Our practical working knowledge, of what societies are and could be, makes us aware of the many ways we need to cooperate with others to achieve our goals, and how they may react negatively to our agendas of societal changes. However, social resistance—which may be overtly antagonistic or subtle but powerful—need not hold us back in our efforts to improve our societies. Our socially intelligent strategies are intrinsically resilient, and often gradually overcome even the strongest initial protests to our visions.

Social intelligence sharpens our visions of societal possibilities with social facts and increased precision. Furthermore, our socially intelligent strategies are effective because they have sufficiently precise formulations, and are directly related to societies' current social realities. Consequently, we depend on social intelligence to continue to guide us in creating more just future societies. We progress toward what others tell us are impossible goals, for example, because we are motivated to do so, because we work cooperatively and effectively with like-minded others, and because we use the precision of social facts to accomplish our goals in the long run.

Precision enhances our dreams, and is necessary for our visions of improved societies to be realized. Thus, precision is not an add-on task, or a superficial trimming atop our day-to-day efforts to reach our goals, but rather the substance of what we are about when we are socially intelligent. Precision in our applications of social intelligence increases our appreciation of social facts, strengthens our objectivity, makes us more aware of the consequences of our value choices, and predictably leads us toward establishing more fulfilling societies in the present and future.

Social Facts

Social facts are social characteristics, events, and patterns of interactions over short or long periods of time that make up the social realities of our societies. For example, we may measure the number of years of formal education that people have received, and the ages they were when they were in schools. When we have sufficient information about trends over periods of ten years or more, we see how patterns in these social facts clarify to what extent education increases or decreases opportunities in societies.

At best, networks of social facts in our societies deepen our understanding of the most significant social realities of families, beliefs, social classes, and cultures. This information and knowledge helps us to compare and contrast different societies in terms of opportunities for members of their populations, as well as to recognize patterns in globalization. Furthermore, centralized information-gathering groups, such as government agencies or issue-oriented non-government organizations, often provide us with fairly accurate trends and tendencies in social facts within and among societies. These social facts enable us to grasp broad pictures of the social realities and social situations in which we are immersed.

The social intelligence of individuals, communities, societies, and international groups derives from social facts. How we absorb, reject, or react to social facts in our local and global social situations also defines who we are, what we think we can accomplish, and what we actually accomplish. Consequently, our social intelligence helps us to assess possibilities in our most meaningful opportunity structures, which ultimately open or close doors for our accomplishments.

Societies need to pay attention to the social facts that their populations experience, because these social realities motivate individuals and groups to contribute constructively or destructively to shared social conditions in societies. Social facts influence the directions of present and future societies, with the result that using social intelligence to change social facts and their impacts may ultimately reverse present and future trends in societies.

For these reasons social facts may not usefully be denied when we are constructing visions of societies' futures. We are successful in creating meaningful visions of better future societies only when our starting points and forward-looking designs relate directly to existing social facts. We not only need clear starting points for formulating and implementing our visions, but we must also check reality through social facts occasionally as we proceed toward our goals. Moreover, we cannot critically assess our efforts and accomplishments to increase the common good and social justice merely by envisioning alternative ways to organize our populations, unless we pay attention to changes in the social facts and social realities of our current social situations.

Social facts are means that increase precision in our aims and accomplishments, while trying to reach goals of choosing our societies and changing our societies. We do not improve our shared social situations unless we have social facts that show that opportunities and resources are more broadly distributed in our societies now than before. The precision that social facts bring to our strategies to better our societies is invaluable, because social facts express the changing social realities within and among our societies.

However, we do not need definitively well-researched social facts to guide our socially intelligent actions at all turns, although such information is significant and useful whenever it is available. More importantly, we need to give serious attention to understanding patterns of contemporary shifts in social trends. For example, reading serious news reports about social facts, as they are lived and experienced in present day social conditions, may be sufficiently clear to usefully inform our socially intelligent actions. Historical information about the social realities of families, beliefs, social classes, and cultures is also an invaluable guide to understanding social needs in our present and future societies. In this way, carefully selected social facts of the past may influence how we change our present societies and choose future societies now.

Social facts increase our objectivity in choosing our societies. Information which describes our social circumstances disciplines our inclinations to distort our thinking when we assess social issues and decide how to respond effectively to our current social situations. Furthermore, social intelligence guides our interpretations of social facts by returning our attention to the power and complexities of the social realities of families, beliefs, social classes, cultures, and societies.

Overall, social facts help us to take more responsible actions as socially intelligent individuals and historical actors. Social facts are ballast for our efforts to change our societies in directions that we truly choose, and social facts inevitably remind us to pay attention to complex and powerful social realities. In so doing, social facts prevent us from making our moral ideals of the common good and social justice too impractical to meet the real needs of our populations. More importantly, social facts are the spirit and essence of our socially intelligent awareness. Social facts enliven the precision of our visions of improved futures by grounding them in social realities, such as available job opportunities, and by changing our societies in realistic directions.

Objectivity

The ideal of objectivity has often been considered as so impersonal that it actually harms human relations. However, objectivity can also free individuals and groups who are trapped in narrow parochial ways of viewing themselves, others, communities, societies, and the world. In fact, to the extent that we see and act only according to our own narrow interests, we cannot at the same time concern ourselves with the well-being of populations in our societies or other societies.

Although in wartime we necessarily heighten our loyalties to our own societies, in times of peace—or when we try to create more peaceful societies for the future—we need to understand and use broad reference points to increase our objectivity. In the long run maintaining objectivity enables us and our societies to contribute more directly and more effectively in collective actions to establish social conditions that achieve lasting peaceful coexistence within and among societies. Objectivity is an essential component of holding constructive broad views of ourselves and our societies, which serve to gradually establish social justice goals.

Social intelligence draws attention to such contrasts in social perspectives, and their impacts on how we think, what we believe, and what we do. Even in focusing primarily on the well-being of individuals, social intelligence encourages us to increase our objectivity about ourselves and our most significant others, in order to think more clearly in long range terms about our personal well-being and the well-being of our societies. As well as serving as a pragmatic social and moral ideal, social intelligence is a technique which broadens our thinking sufficiently to see more options in how to create and live together meaningfully in improved future societies.

When we value social intelligence, and try to increase our social intelligence on a daily basis, we increase our objectivity. For example, we free ourselves from inordinately tight and restrictive loyalties to traditional or past value choices, in order to express socially intelligent values such as equality, inclusiveness, diversity, cooperation, and openness today and tomorrow. By experimenting with how we live more meaningfully according to these socially intelligent values, we learn that we must respect others' value choices as well as our own, and that these better ways to choose and achieve our goals are possible.

Objectivity, like social intelligence, is a means to achieve the goal of deliberately choosing which societies we want to move toward now for the future. At the same time, objectivity is a tool which increases our social intelligence and helps us to live more meaningfully. For example, we see our options more clearly—for ourselves and our societies— when we use the broad perspectives of social intelligence to increase our objectivity.

Objectivity helps us to understand that there are important nuances in social realities that can be changed, even through individual efforts. However, objectivity also shows us that the results of individual efforts to change our societies are consistently more effective when we consider the views of all members of our societies, especially when we work cooperatively and collectively with others to accomplish these changes. Learning social intelligence includes learning how to be objective, and learning how to work collectively to achieve the common good and social justice.

Objectivity increases our awareness of social facts and their importance in social realities that need to be changed, in order to open up more opportunities and possibilities for the future. We assess social facts in our communities and societies more accurately and more effectively when we are objective in our approaches, thinking, and goals. For example, objectivity requires us to consider the well-being of whole societies rather than the vested interests of a few members of our populations, and objectivity also requires us to see our societies as participants in relentless currents of globalization.

Deliberately cultivating objectivity increases our social intelligence, so that we are more aware and more responsible historical actors. Objectivity promotes ways of seeing the world that coordinate efforts effectively between diverse groups within and among societies, because objectivity is grounded in social facts. In these respects objectivity enhances our enlightenment about how we meet existential challenges to survive and be fulfilled in our societies today, especially by connecting who we are to what we want to accomplish now and in the future.

Value Choices

Whatever choices we make about our present and future societies—whether we choose these societies individually or collectively—we at the same time make value choices that relate directly to ourselves as well as to our present and future societies. For example, when we focus on creating visions of societies that we want to bring into existence, or on the precision we need to develop means to make our visions possible, we must also make significant value choices in order to progress effectively. Moreover, our examinations of social facts, as well as our capacities to remain objective in these endeavors, depend on the values we cultivate, espouse, and integrate through our actions.

Social intelligence heightens our awareness about the varieties of societies that have existed through time. In modern societies, which usually have rich historical sources of information, we can sometimes trace trends in the evolution of societies in our earliest communities, traditional societies, and modern industrial societies based on global market economies. Reviewing this dazzling range of views of how societies have been in the past, and are in the present for the future, is a valuable starting point for assessing which societies we choose now.

Social intelligence shows us that our historical pasts need not determine how we live in the present or future. However, an important social intelligence principle is that today's societies have destructive social problems and contentious social issues in part because insufficient attention is given to how existing resources and opportunities are distributed within and among societies. Therefore, being socially intelligent as historical actors requires us to focus more on meeting the social needs of entire populations, than on meeting the needs of elites such as privileged upper social classes.

Although social intelligence is a moral ideal in its own right, it does not emphasize the significance of its working principles for moral reasons, even though important ethical views often guide deliberations about existential social issues such as equal rights or social fulfillment. Rather, social intelligence is markedly pragmatic about assessing the ultimate well-being and fulfillment of whole populations and the world. A socially intelligent principle here is that when we manage ourselves so that we increase community cooperation rather than alienation, we will be able to prevent some extremes in social deprivation and intense political conflicts such as wars.

Social intelligence is working knowledge that derives from our observations and understanding of how and why individuals, groups, and societies interact, and of how and why particular social realities exist. For example, when we increase our social intelligence, we are more able to see constructive possibilities for peaceful coexistence among social classes and societies. However, heightening our awareness in these respects is not sufficient. We can only be truly socially intelligent when we make strategic use of social intelligence in our everyday choices, decisions, and actions, especially in how we choose societies in the present for the future.

Social intelligence principles suggest that even though stark contrasts among societies' different cultures necessarily continue to exist, meeting social needs to have equal opportunities, to be inclusive, to embrace diversity, to cooperate, and to be open with each other will eventually create better societies. Furthermore, when we choose to express social and cultural values of equality, inclusiveness, diversity, cooperation, and openness in our interactions, our shared goals to create more constructive societies are gradually accomplished.

In these respects social intelligence views constructive value choices as being based on deep individual and social needs to survive and be fulfilled. Consequently, social intelligence encourages us to make value choices that reinforce equality, inclusiveness, diversity, cooperation, and openness, because these values meet vital needs of individuals and societies in the long run. For example, the social and cultural values of equality, inclusiveness, diversity, cooperation, and openness create more productive ways to relate to each other, sustain alternatives to social classes, and construct new societies that have not yet been experienced in history and evolution.

When we use value choices to be more aware, enlightened, and deliberate in establishing equality, inclusiveness, diversity, cooperation, and openness in whatever we do each day, we make progress in creating more humane societies in the present for the future. Just as civilizations preserved different values in the past, we make new value choices today to predictably enhance social relations in the long run. For example, we base our individual and collective actions on new visions, increased precision, meaningful social facts, and thoughtful objectivity. Thus, social intelligence guides us to accomplish complex significant goals today for our present and future societies.

Societies and Fulfillment

Social issues involved in both changing our societies and choosing our societies call up existential questions about which societies are possible. In order to arrive at practical answers to this question, we must make some critical assumptions about the nature of human nature, such as whether the political and emotional impacts of our current societies allow members of their populations to be fulfilled. Social intelligence helps us to think through these major concerns, so that we do not waste our time and energy by pursuing empty ideals, but rather focus on real possibilities and effective strategies that serve us well for choosing societies and changing societies.

Social intelligence principles open some doors of possibilities and close others. To the extent that we are committed to applying only the most constructive uses of social intelligence to improve ourselves and our societies, we see from historical facts that societies can bring fulfillment to their populations rather than manipulate or coerce them to satisfy the narrow vested interests of elites. For example, history teaches us that democracy has revolutionized many societies, but that democracy still needs our support and participation in order to increase fulfillment for more societies in the present and future.

Principles of social intelligence guide us in our individual and collective efforts to achieve democracy and social justice because they are grounded in social facts and the practical knowledge of social realities. For example, when we combine our visions of better futures for societies and members of their populations with paying close attention to social facts and objectivity about choosing societies, we are more likely to make value choices that improve societies

XII. Choosing Societies

and bring about fulfillment. Choosing to express equality, inclusiveness, diversity, cooperation, and openness in our societies at all times ensures that the societies we choose and change have enhanced capacities to bring fulfillment to all members of their populations.

We ensure that our efforts to move in these directions—individually and collectively—are effective and worthwhile for most by concentrating on the five major social influences and social realities in our societies: families, beliefs, social classes, cultures, and societies. When we are awake to the power and complexities of these five basic social influences, we are more effective in our efforts to change societies and choose societies. For example, we largely avoid unintentionally spinning our wheels by getting trapped into attaining goals that essentially maintain the status quo of societies and social classes.

When we observe families, beliefs, social classes, cultures, and societies more carefully, we create foundations for understanding social intelligence and for interacting with families, beliefs, social classes, cultures, and societies more freely. Furthermore, seeing the significance of social intelligence in our everyday lives helps us to consolidate social facts, which deepen our appreciation of the power and complexities of families, beliefs, social classes, cultures, and societies. This process makes us more discriminating because we now associate what had seemed to be external social influences with our identities and agencies as human beings. Consequently, we consider more seriously who we are and how we act in relation to the largely emotion-driven social forces of families, beliefs, social classes, cultures, and societies.

At best, social intelligence frees us from being dominated by others' expectations and goals. When we understand—through social intelligence—that it is possible for us to decide who we are and what we want to accomplish more authentically, we use social intelligence principles to make new value choices and go in new directions. As we become more responsible historical actors, we cooperate with others more openly and more effectively to choose and change our societies. For example, we participate in building more benign social structures that benefit all members of populations rather than social class elites.

Becoming more socially intelligent is a lifetime endeavor that increases our fulfillment and others' fulfillment. Even when the social conditions of our particular social situations continue to be alienating, social intelligence helps us to create more secure and more meaningful foundations for our identities, especially by participating in our families differently. Furthermore, when we work with others to choose and change our societies more deliberately, we free ourselves so that we can deal with significant global issues like creating an international community that fulfills more widespread needs in various populations.

Suggested Reading

Barlow, Andrew L., ed. 2007. *Collaborations for Social Justice: Professionals, Publics, and Policy Change.* Lanham, MD: Rowman & Littlefield.

Berger, Peter. 1963. *Invitation to Sociology.* New York: Doubleday.

Cesari, Jocelyne. 2006. *When Islam and Democracy Meet: Muslims in Europe and in the United States.* New York, NY: Palgrave.

Chang, Grace. 2000. *Disposable Domestics: Immigrant Women Workers in the Global Economy.* Boston, MA: South End Press.

Domhoff, G. William. 1998. *Who Rules America?* Mountain View, CA: Mayfield Publishing.

Du Bois, W. E. B. 1994/1903. *The Souls of Black Folk.* New York: Dover Publications.

Ehrenreich, Barbara. 2001. *Nickel and Dimed: On (Not) Getting By in America.* New York: Metropolitan Books.

Finkelstein, Marvin S. 2004. *Net-Works: Workplace Change in the Global Economy: A Critical and Practical Guide.* Lanham, MD: Rowman & Littlefield.

Friedman, Thomas L. 1999. *The Lexus and the Olive Tree.* New York: Farrar Straus & Giroux.

Gans, Herbert J. 1999. *Popular Culture and High Culture: An Analysis and Evaluation of Taste.* New York: Basic Books.

Gat, Azar. 2006. *War in Human Civilization.* Oxford, UK: Oxford University Press.

Gitlin, Todd. 2002. *Media Unlimited: How the Torrent of Images and Sound Overwhelms Our Lives.* New York: Metropolitan Books.

Griswold, Wendy. 1994. *Cultures and Societies in a Changing World.* Thousand Oaks, CA: Pine Forge.

Harris, Paul G., and Patricia D. Siplon, eds. 2007. *The Global Politics of AIDS.* Boulder, CO: Lynne Rienner.

Hennock, E. P. 2007. *The Origin of the Welfare State in England and Germany, 1850-1914: Social Policies Compared.* New York, NY: Cambridge University Press.

Higley, John, and Michael Burton. 2006. *Elite Foundations of Liberal Democracy.* Lanham, MD: Rowman & Littlefield.

Ingstad, Benedicte, and Susan Reynolds, eds. 2007. *Disability in Local and Global Worlds.* Berkeley, CA: University of California Press.

Layton, Robert. 2006. *Order and Anarchy: Civil Society, Social Disorder and War.* NewYork, NY: Cambridge University Press.

Louie, Miriam Ching Yoon. 2001. *Sweatshop Warriors: Immigrant Women Workers Take on the Global Factory.* Cambridge, MA: South End Press.

Mills, C. Wright. 1959. *The Sociological Imagination.* New York: Oxford University Press.

Oliver, Melvin L., and Thomas M. Shapiro. 1995. *Black Wealth/White Wealth: A New Perspective on Racial Inequality.* New York: Routledge.

Reiman, Jeffrey. 2002. *The Rich Get Richer and the Poor Get Prison?* Needham Heights, MA: Allyn and Bacon.

Roberts, J. Timmons, and Bradley C. Parks. 2006. *A Climate of Injustice: Global Inequality, North-South Politics, and Climate Policy.* Cambridge, MA: The MIT Press.

Turner, Bryan S. 2006. *Vulnerability and Human Rights.* University Park, PA: The Pennsylvania State University Press.

With many thanks to my colleagues in the Georgetown University Sociology Department; the Bowen Center for the Study of the Family; the Association for Applied and Clinical Sociology; and Research Committee #46 on Clinical Sociology, the International Sociological Association. I am also indebted to my clients and students, who have taught me so much, and of course to my wonderful American and English families, who continue to stand by me on a daily basis.